Craft & Community

Traditional Arts in Contemporary Society

An exhibition organized by the Museum of the
Balch Institute for Ethnic Studies and the
Pennsylvania Heritage Affairs Commission

Edited by Shalom D. Staub

The exhibition is generously supported by a grant from
the National Endowment for the Humanities,
a federal agency

In celebration of the American Folklore Society
Centennial

1888-89
AMERICAN
FOLKLORE
SOCIETY
CENTENNIAL
1988-89

Kutztown, PA 19530
(215) 683-5820

Craft and Community:
Traditional Arts in Contemporary Society

December 15, 1988 – February 24, 1989:	The Balch Institute for Ethnic Studies, Philadelphia, PA
April 1 – May 28, 1989	Luckenbach Mill Gallery, Historic Bethlehem, Inc., Bethlehem, PA
July 8 – September 10, 1989	Roberson Center for Arts and Sciences, Binghamton, NY
October 6 – November 15, 1989	Hershey Museum of American Life, Hershey, PA
February 18 – April 8, 1990	Erie Museum of Art, Erie, PA
May 20 – July 22, 1990	Palmer Museum of Art, The Pennsylvania State University, State College, PA
August 29 – November 2, 1990	University Art Gallery, University of Pittsburgh, Pittsburgh, PA
January 10 – March 18, 1991	Old Bedford Village, Bedford, PA

Table of Contents

745
STA

11.588

Foreword
Mark S. Singel, Lieutenant Governor, Commonwealth of Pennsylvania

As Lieutenant Governor and Chairman of the Pennsylvania Heritage Affairs Commission, I welcome you to the Commission's first major exhibition, "Craft and Community: Traditional Arts in Contemporary Society." The exhibition captures the spirit of Pennsylvania: its ethnic diversity, its distinctive regions, its rural and urban communities and their values of hard work, pride of place, and joy of celebration.

Traveling throughout our Commonwealth, one encounters an amazing variety of cultural traditions. Those represented in the exhibition reflect the origins of present-day Pennsylvanians—from Europe, Africa, Asia, and the Americas. The exhibition highlights occupations of these immigrants when they settled—coal mining, logging, furniture making, and stone carving, among many others—and showcases the traditions of community which contribute to the richness of Pennsylvania life.

These traditions do more than reflect the countries and cultures of our ancestors. They combine with the people and experiences of the New World to create a way of life that is distinctively Pennsylvanian. "Craft and Community" provides an opportunity to explore and celebrate the richness of cultural pluralism in Pennsylvania, a diversity of voices with a common expression.

Ever since Europeans (and later Africans and Asians) began to settle North America, the question of "what is an American" has intrigued both native and foreign observers. Because so many ethnic groups have either come here, or have evolved in our midst, our society reflects the cultures of the world. On the other hand, the various ethnic cultures that do exist in the United States are no longer the same as they were in the Old World. They have changed because every ethnic group that has come here has abandoned certain cultural characteristics, it has borrowed others already found here, and it has preserved still others that it considers to be vital to its identity.

"Craft and Community" speaks to our cultural diversity. In the everyday household artifacts on display here the discerning observer will see how various cultures have changed over time. While this exhibit does not answer the question "what is an American," it makes a stab at doing so by pointing to our ever-changing cultural makeup. As long as newcomers continue to arrive at our shores, our culture will keep changing. Perhaps this is what is so unique about the United States — its receptivity to change and its unwillingness to ossify its national characteristics. It may be too dynamic to do so and herein may lie its true genius.

M. Mark Stolarik
President
The Balch Institute for
Ethnic Studies

Acknowledgements

The Balch Institute for Ethnic Studies and The Pennsylvania Heritage Affairs Commission are grateful to many people and institutions for their efforts on behalf of "Craft and Community." The generous support of the National Endowment for the Humanities (NEH) a federal agency, made the exhibition and catalog possible. The National Endowment for the Arts (NEA) has provided funding for the program series which will accompany the exhibition on its statewide tour. In addition, the William Penn Foundation, the Institute for Museum Services and the City of Philadelphia supported the museum's exhibition program for 1988.

Dr. Shalom Staub, now Executive Director of the Pennsylvania Heritage Affairs Commission, initiated the project and secured funding for it while he served the Commission as Director of State Folklife Programs. As Guest Curator, he selected the case studies and objects for the exhibition and guided their interpretation. He also served as catalog editor as well as a contributor. Amy Skillman provided critical organizational assistance after succeeding Staub as Director of State Folklife Programs in May of 1988. Working closely with Dr. James F. Turk, Director of Education at The Balch Institute, and with representatives of the other host institutions for the exhibition, Skillman also coordinated the program series accompanying the tour.

Two years of preliminary field survey work in Pennsylvania were supported through planning grants from the NEH, the NEA and the Pennsylvania Council on the Arts, a state agency. The folklorists who participated in this initial phase were: Carole Boughter, Deborah Bowman, Dr. Doris Dyen, Dr. Harry Gammerdinger, Dr. Thomas E. Graves, Dr. Malachi O'Connor, Dr. Shalom Staub, Ruth Tonachel and Richard Vidutis. Additional fieldwork, dedicated to preparing the exhibition case studies and writing the essays in this catalog, was undertaken by Dyen, Graves, O'Connor and Vidutis, along with Dr. J. Joseph Edgette, Susan L. F. Isaacs, Dr. Geraldine Johnson, Sally Peterson and John Reynolds.

The project's Advisory Board provided critical guidance and assistance throughout all stages: Dr. Simon Bronner, folklorist, Pennsylvania State University, Harrisburg; Dr. Richard Chalfen, anthropologist, Temple University, Philadelphia; Jeannette Lasansky, art historian, Union County Oral Traditions Project, Lewisburg, Pennsylvania; Dr. Chris Musello, independent scholar and filmmaker, Salisbury, Maryland; Dr. Scott Swank, art historian, Winterthur Museum, Winterthur, Delaware; Dr. Robert Teske, folklorist, Cedarburg Cultural Center, Cedarburg, Wisconsin and Dr. M. Mark Stolarik, historian (President, The Balch Institute for Ethnic Studies).

We are especially grateful to the talented craftsworkers who have generously lent samples of their craft to the touring exhibition for a period of 3 years: Allison Park Quiltmakers; Osvaldo Ayala; Margaret Bardonner; Aguedo Beltran; Judith Brandau; Terrence Cameron; Lucille Cardone; John Claypoole; Robert A. Demarest; Felician Sisters of Holy Trinity Church, Erie; Ernest S. Gabler; Sheila Graham; Ivan Hoyt; Marijka Jula; Michael Jula; Michael Kapeluck; Kapeluck family; Helen Kolling; Susan Leviton; Foua Lo; Yee Vang Lo; Yer Lo; Chia Ker Lor; Isaac Maefield; Lhee Moua; Mai Doua Moua; Mao Moua; Pa Houa Moua, Robert C. Moore; Lewis Reinhart; Bob Rock; Bill Schuster; Robbie Seibert; Lee Moua Sirirathasuk; Pang Xiong Sirirathasuk; Fonda Smith; Michael Stephano; Mary Margaret Sullivan; Harry Thompson; Becky Vasgaard; Lee Woida; Mary Lou Wolff; Harvard C. Wood, III; Ka Xiong; Mai Xiong Chang; Mao Vang Xiong; Yer Xiong; Bao Yang, Jr.; Bao Yang, Sr.; Shai Yang; Joseph J. Zebrowski; and Aaron Zook.

Other lenders to the exhibition include: Monsignor John Daniszewski, Holy Trinity Church, Erie; Danielle Brandau; Mai Xiong Chang; Thomas E. Graves; Susan L.F. Isaacs; Margaret Mills; the Orthodox Monastery of the Holy Transfiguration, Ellwood City; Sally Peterson; the Philadelphia Museum of Art; Charlotte Schuster; the Spanish-American Civic Association, Lancaster and Darrell G. Spencer. (Loans from the Philadelphia Art Museum were included in the Philadelphia installation only.)

The following craftsworkers are represented from the collections of the museum of the Balch Institute: Ruthanne Hartung, Joseph Janco, Jr., Annie Morgalis, Frank Valentich, and workers in numerous Lancaster county Amish and Mennonite carriage shops. The Pennsylvania Heritage Affairs Commission lent ethnographic photographs from its archives.

Steven Tucker, exhibition designer, found creative solutions to the challenge of presenting a multitude of diverse forms with strong visual coherence. Joan Guerin inventively designed the exhibition catalog, and, with Graphica, the accompanying poster and brochure. Charles Adams, Gregory Zeitlin and Allison Zito assisted in the show's fabrication and installation. Paula Benkart provided insightful copy editing for the catalog. Museum intern Davina Robinson ably assisted me in the preparation of the artifact checklist. Jennifer Gardner, Rosalie Robinson and Diane Zatz offered technical assistance in the production of the catalog. The ethnographic photographs included in the catalog are by Doris Dyen, J. Joseph Edgette, Thomas E. Graves, Michael E. Haritan, Susan L. F. Isaacs, Geraldine Johnson, Sally Peterson, John Reynolds, Shalom Staub, Richard Vidutis, Mike Worley (Commonwealth Media Services), and Mai Xiong Chang. Will Brown and Anthony C. Kambic photographed the objects. (Additional ethnographic photos in the exhibition are by John Abrams.) Dave Marshall of Keener Offset and Lou Rambo of Graphic Arts Composition provided guidance and assistance in catalog production.

Ben Levin skillfully produced the accompanying videotapes of craftsworkers with the assistance of Eliat Goldman, Wayne Derrick, Michael Bailey and Eugene Martin. Others who generously offered advice and assistance include: Pamela B. Nelson and Elizabeth Holland of the museum staff; Suzi Jones (NEH); Bess Lomax Hawes and Barry Bergey (NEA); Robert Wilburn, The Carnegie, Pittsburgh; Randall Snyder, Lancaster County Historical Society; Bea Garvan, Jack Lindsay, Ann Percy and Conna Clark of the Philadelphia Museum of Art; Tom McCabe and Catherine Jacobs of the Folklife Center of International House of Philadelphia; Jonathan Cox and Gail Getz of the State Museum, Harrisburg; Shawn Aubitz of the National Archives, Mid-Atlantic Region; Johnny Irizarry of Taller Puertorriqueño; and the staff of the host institutions for the exhibition tour: Joan Lardner Paul and Janet Goloub, Luckenback Mill Gallery, Historic Bethlehem, Inc.; Robert W. Aber and Catherine Schwoeffermann, Roberson Center for the Arts and Sciences; Mary Houts, Eliza Cope Harrison and Tanya Richter, Hershey Museum of American Life; Sanford Sivitz Shaman, Randy Ploog and Charles Garorian, Palmer Museum of Art, The Pennsylvania State University; David Wilkins and Anne L. Helmreich, University Art Gallery, University of Pittsburgh; Robert K. Sweet and John Bennett, Old Bedford Village; and John Vanco, Erie Art Museum.

We are very grateful to all of those involved in the exhibition and related programming for their enthusiastic support of the project.

Gail F. Stern
Museum Director,
The Balch Institute for Ethnic Studies
Associate Director, Craft and Community

Notes on Contributors

Dr. Doris J. Dyen is a freelance folklife consultant who has worked closely with the Pennsylvania Heritage Affairs Commission on numerous projects. Prior to her moving to Pittsburgh, she served as Folklife Specialist for the Florida Folklife Program.

Dr. J. Joseph Edgette is a professor of English and director of the Masters in Liberal Studies Program at Widener University. His folklore research and publications have focused on gravestones and carvers in Pennsylvania.

Dr. Thomas E. Graves is a freelance folklife consultant who has worked closely with the Pennsylvania Heritage Affairs Commission. His folklore research has focused on Pennsylvania German traditions, particularly hex sign painting and folk medicine.

Susan L. F. Isaacs is a Ph.D. candidate at the University of Pennsylvania's Department of Folklore and Folklife. Her dissertation examines contemporary redware potters in the Pennsylvania German tradition.

Dr. Malachi S. O'Connor is a freelance folklife consultant with extensive fieldwork experience in Pennsylvania, New Jersey and New York. His recently completed dissertation examined innovation in the design, construction and use of tools.

Sally Peterson is a Ph.D. candidate at the University of Pennsylvania's Department of Folklore and Folklife. Since 1983, her research has focused on textile traditions within the Hmong communities of the United States.

John Reynolds is a Cultural Arts Specialist with the National Parks Service at the Cuyahoga Valley National Recreation Area, Ohio. From 1985-1987, he was Director of the Folklife Center of International House, Philadelphia, where he conducted fieldwork among Philadelphia's many ethnic communities.

Dr. Shalom D. Staub is the executive director of the Pennsylvania Heritage Affairs Commission. From 1982-87, he served on the Commission's staff as Director of State Folklife Programs.

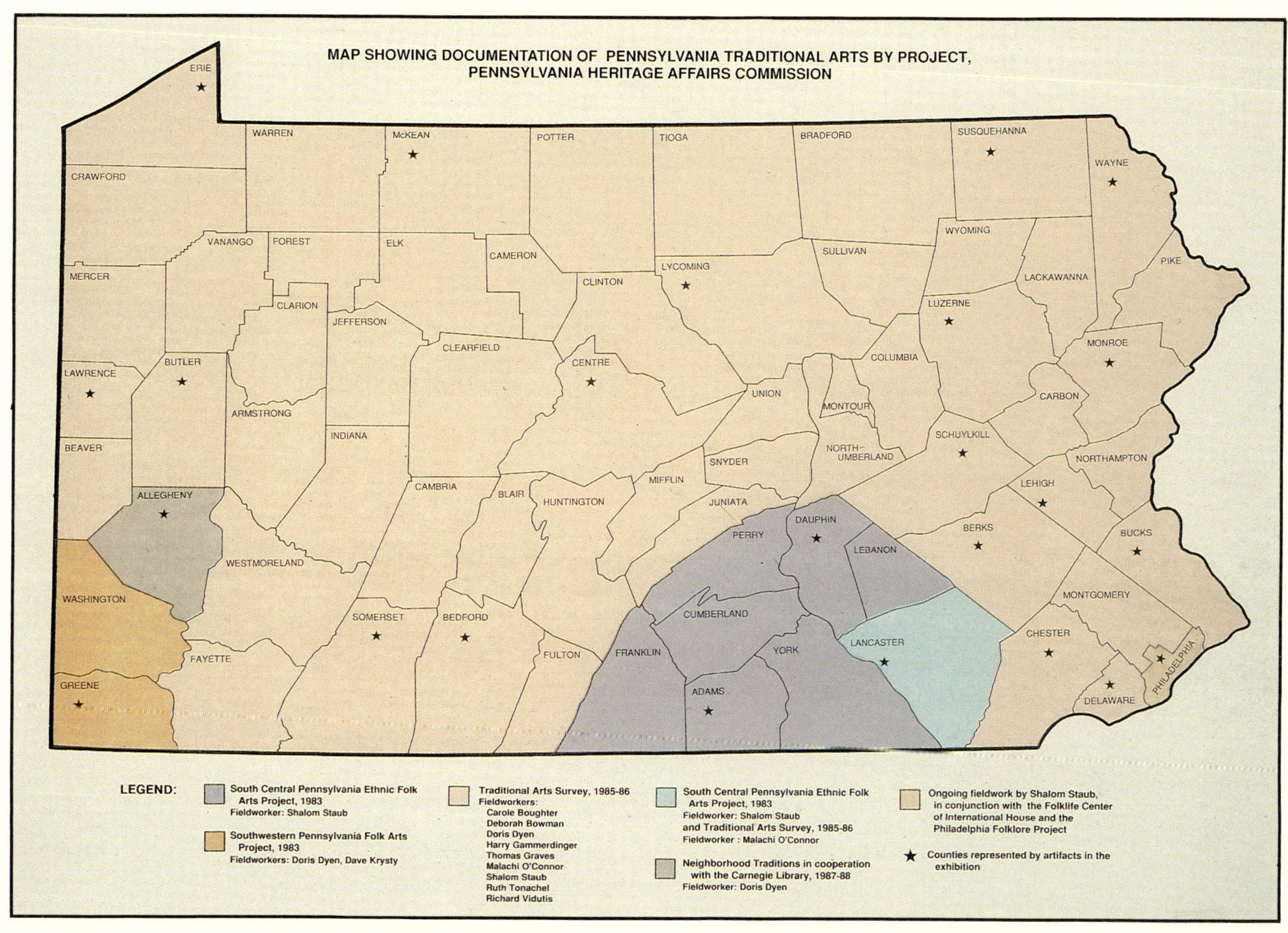

Color Plate #1

(Color Plate #2):
Hex sign artist John Claypoole perches on a ladder
to paint a new hex sign on
a Pennsylvania barn.
Berks County, 1985.

(Color Plate #3):
At the far end of a work-bench covered with banjo parts and metal bending tools, Bob Rock uses a wooden clamp of his own design to hold a hand saw in his vise while hand sharpening the saw's teeth with a file. Everett, 1988.

Left (Color Plate #4):
Lenni Lenape shirt (checklist #55); breechcloth (checklist #54); leggings (checklist #56); garter tabs (checklist #57); moccasins (checklist #53); and trail bag (checklist #48) by Robert C. Moore

Below (Color Plate #5):
Belt buckle by Robert C. Moore (checklist #49)

Left (Color Plate #6):
Cuatro by Aguedo Beltran
(checklist #60)

Right (Color Plate #7):
Prim by Frank Valentich
(checklist #61)

(Color Plate #8):
"Laurel Wreath" quilt by
Fonda Smith (checklist
#62)

(Color Plate #9):
Summer Wheat Harvest by
Aaron Zook (checklist
#101)

(Color Plate #10):
Amish hooked rug
(checklist #103)

Above (Color Plate #11): Ukrainian *pysanky* (eggs showing stages in the "wax resist" production process), (checklist #147)

Left (Color Plate #12): Ukrainian *pysanky* (decorated eggs) by Michael Kapeluck (clockwise from top center: checklist #140, #143, #144 and #142)

(Color Plate #13): Easter basket with *krashanka* (ritual egg; checklist #139), candle (checklist #138), *paska* (egg bread; checklist #136) and *servetka* (ritual cloth; checklist #137)

(Color Plate #14):
Pysanky: "Geometric"
(checklist #145) and "Ikon
of St. Michael" (checklist
#146)

(Color Plate #15):
Paj ntaub ("story cloth") illustrating the escape of the Hmong to refugee camps in Thailand (checklist #170)

(Color Plate #16): Hmong
apprenticeship sampler
quilt (checklist #172)

(Color Plate #17):
Mask by Osvaldo Ayala
(checklist #12)

(Color Plate #18):
Icon of St. John the Theo-
logian by a sister of the
Orthodox Monastery of the
Holy Transfiguration
(checklist #8)

(Color Plate #19):
Jewish *Ketubah* (marriage
contract) by Susan Leviton
(checklist #7)

Left:
Christening ensemble by
Judith Brandau (checklist
#10)

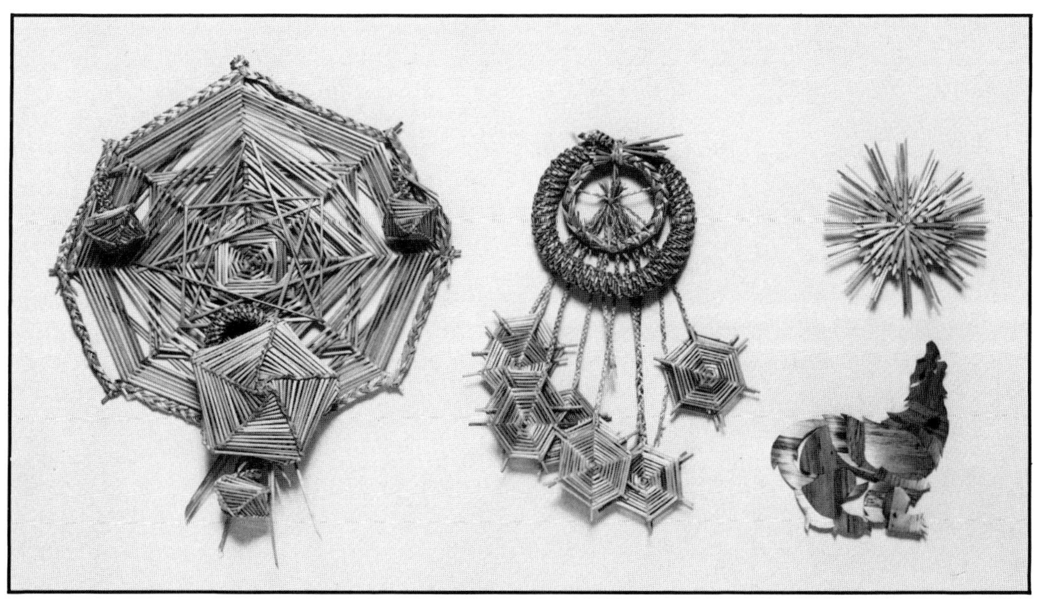

Left:
Christmas ornaments by
Annie Morgalis
(checklist #15)

Left:
"Fire engine" funeral sculpture by Joseph Janco, Sr.
and Joseph Janco, Jr.
(checklist #11)

Below:
Pennsylvania longrifle by
Joseph J. Zebrowski
(checklist #1)

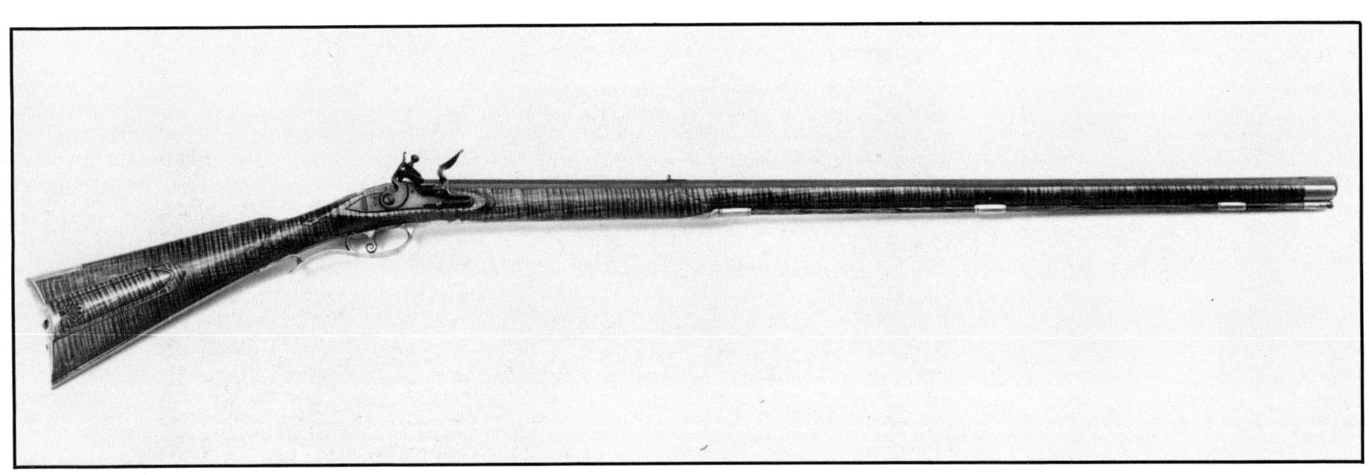

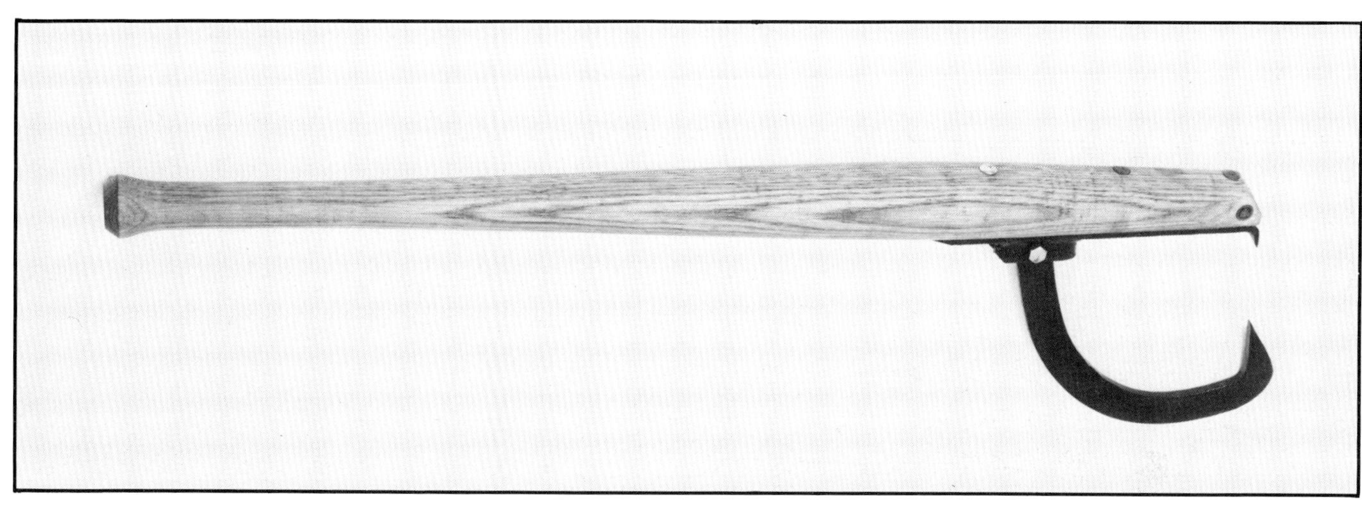

Above:
Cant hook by Michael Stephano (checklist #6)

Right:
Carving of a mine shaft entrance by Harry Thompson (checklist #16)

Left:
Basket by Lewis Reinhart
(checklist #13)

Below:
Walking stick by Isaac
Maefield (checklist #2)

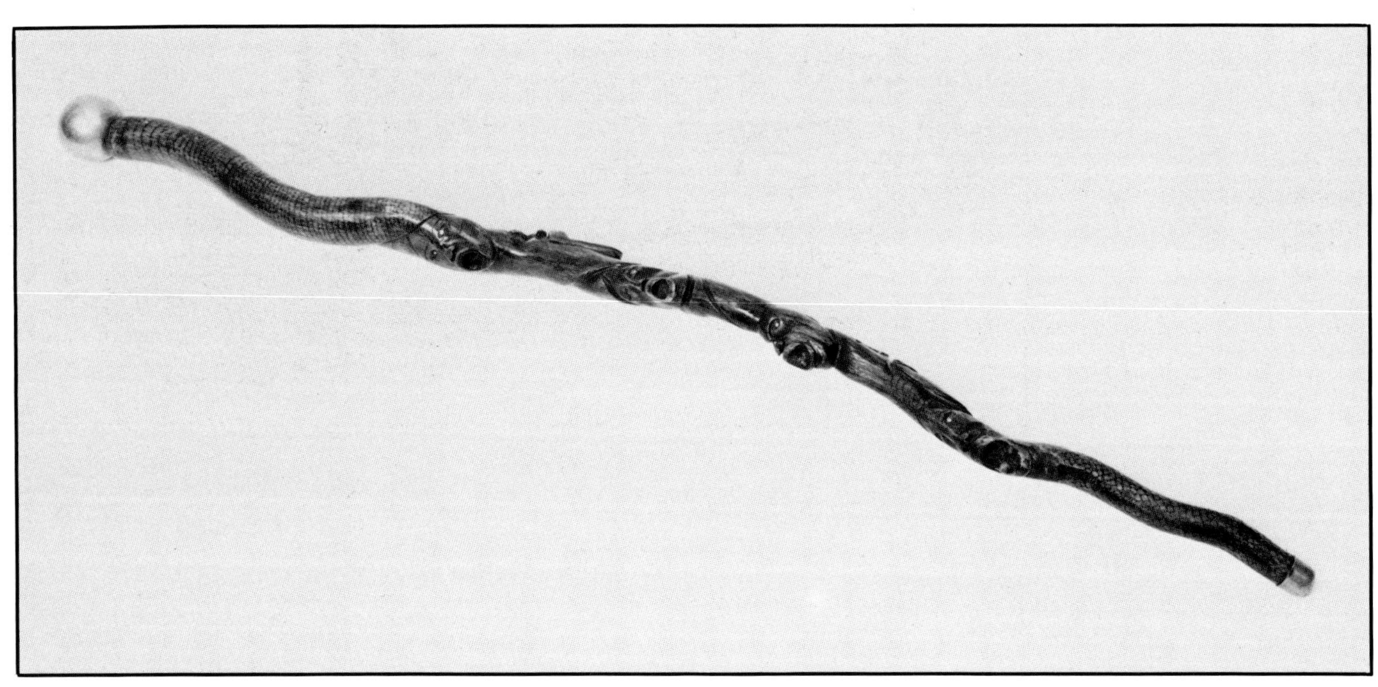

Right:
Carved chain (checklist #4)
and "ball in cage" (checklist
#5) by Robert A. Demarest

Right:
Valley Belle of Pittsburgh
by Ernest S. Gabler
(checklist #14)

Left:
Nebo Lutheran Church by
Becky S. Vasgaard
(checklist #3)

TRADITIONAL CRAFTSMANSHIP IN PENNSYLVANIA:
An Ethnographic Perspective

Shalom D. Staub

Consider the following objects: a longrifle, an Afro-American walking stick, a Pennsylvania German-style paper cut depicting a hundred-year-old Swedish church in rural northwestern Pennsylvania, a carved wooden chain and "ball in cage," a cant hook used to roll logs, a Jewish marriage contract with calligraphy and illumination, an Eastern Orthodox icon, an embroidered christening ensemble, a Slovak wire sculpture for displaying flowers at a funeral, a willow basket, a Puerto Rican coconut mask, a Lithuanian straw Christmas-tree ornament, a model of a western Pennsylvania riverboat, and an anthracite-coal sculpture.

In recent years, many handcrafted artifacts such as these have achieved prominence and popularity as folk art. Dealers, collectors, art historians, folklorists, museums, and retail outlets each have contributed a particular perspective in attempting to define the phenomenon. The result has been a definitional quagmire. Just what is "folk art," and what is meant by "traditional crafts"?

Popular notions of folk art have been heavily influenced by the world of fine art. Interest in folk art can be traced to nineteenth- and twentieth-century artists and craftsworkers who rebelled against some of the principles of academic art. They embraced instead what they considered to be the simple, direct forms and designs found among the "folk" in order to legitimize their own use of simplified shapes, arbitrary perspective, and unmixed color.[1] This approach has emphasized the artist's lack of formal training, and the primitive, naive, idiosyncratic, even childlike quality of such work. These characteristics are quite misleading, for they define a "folk artist" by what the artist does not know, using criteria for evaluation external to the artist's own experience.[2] Folk art, so defined is the product of a twentieth-century aesthetic movement and, more recently, of commercial interests which have granted common objects the status of "art," worthy of being collected and displayed, bought and sold. The contemporary fascination with "folk art" represents the crossing of boundaries between multiple "art worlds," the discovery and re-valuation by an art establishment of objects produced by those outside the conventions of its own art world.[3]

An ethnographic approach to folk art provides a valuable alternative perspective. It seeks to understand material objects in the social context of the lives of the craftsworkers and their customers. Emphasizing native definitions for "art" or "craft" based on the shared values and forms of particular cultural traditions, the ethnographic approach considers questions of cultural meaning, significance, and aesthetics.

The differences between these definitions and perspectives on folk art have tremendous implications for the display and interpretation of artifacts in exhibitions. Many folk art exhibitions have been patterned after the familiar installations of fine art in which the object "speaks for itself." Curators who think that the viewer should not be distracted from directly experiencing an object arrange isolated artifacts in attractive cases and wall displays accompanied by labels which identify the piece's classification, provenance, dimensions and owner.

On the other hand, ethnographers argue that such installations offer the viewer little understanding of the aesthetics, values, motivations, and concerns of either the individuals who made the objects or of the communities that supported the artist's activity by using the objects. Rather than isolating artifacts from social experience, ethnographic interpretation in the museum seeks to show the viewer the integration of artifact and social life. Objects are presented in relation to each other, and photo documentation and text panels offer ethnographic details concerning the contexts and patterns of production and use. The people who infuse the objects with life are a significant focus of attention in photographs and in texts which derive from field research. Interpretive programming, such as crafts demonstrations and workshops in the museum, also plays a special role in ethnographic presentation.

To lay the groundwork for "Craft and Community: Traditional Arts in Contemporary Society," the Pennsylvania Heritage Affairs Commission undertook a series of fieldwork-based documentation projects throughout the state to identify living cultural traditions based on shared ethnicity, region, religion, or occupation (see Color Plate #1). The skills and knowledge that support such traditions are learned and transmitted in informal, face-to-face interaction through observation, imitation, and repetition. The Commission's efforts have identified thousands of traditional artists and craftsworkers whose creative expressions are vitally important in their own lives and in the lives of their communities.

This exhibition draws upon ethnographic perspectives to present an "insider's view." The majority of items have been lent by the craftsworkers themselves or by members of their communities. With their guidance, objects were selected on the basis of social context, not for their established status as "folk art" by virtue of being in a museum or private collection. This approach represents a radical departure from that of many folk art exhibitions around the country, and it reflects a major shift away from the attitudes of folk art collectors to the approach of folklorists who explore what people in local communities consider to be their own folk art traditions.[4]

The term "folk art" is not used prominently in this exhibition in order to avoid the problematic associations of that term. "Craft" is used in its place to emphasize both the acquired knowledge of the craftsworker and the process of making objects. Using craft as our key concept more clearly reflects the way the people we encountered think about and discuss their own activities. Nevertheless, our use of craft in no way minimizes the artistic dimension of their work, for elements of design and aesthetic judgment are implicit and clear.[5]

Below:
The clamping jig (center) is used to join wheel spokes to the center hub and align the spokes to receive each half of the wheel rim. An air-powered drill is used to tighten bolts. Lancaster County, 1988.

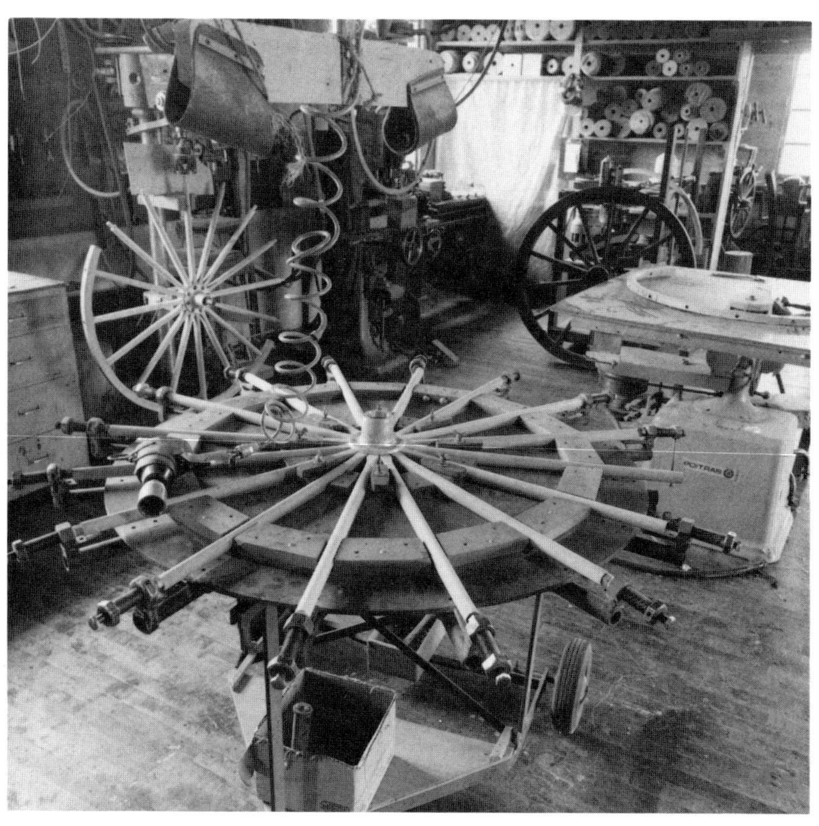

The objects in "Craft and Community" are not idiosyncratic; they represent the work of individuals who are connected to communities with shared craft and aesthetic traditions. To make sense of these artifacts, the exhibition gives primary attention to the craftsworkers themselves in order to reveal the complex relationships of people, objects, and social meaning. Folklorist Charles Camp addressed these relationships in his "Diagnostic Report" on traditional craftsmanship in America:

> Traditional craftsworkers generally practice their craft within the communities to which they were born and within which they exercise a great number of inherited and acquired roles. These roles are in turn shaped by the commonly shared attitudes and expectations of community members regarding the form and function of everyday objects, the symbolic language in which such objects participate, and the spiritual and social construction of the world in which all people (and objects) live.[6]

"Tradition," in the sense I use it here, is rooted in social life.[7] Objects are not in themselves "traditional." Neither age nor lineage alone confers this attribute on an artifact. The tradition is not in the artifact itself, but rather it lies in relationships. Specifically, tradition stems both from the relationship between present experience and the past—between the object and its historical antecedents, between the craftsworker and preceding generations, and between the community and its historical memory; and from relationships within the present—between artifact and maker, between maker and user, and between craftsworker and community. Traditions are constantly recreated, renewed, and relived as individuals and communities "traditionalize" aspects of their experience to create

Above:
(Left to right): Mary Lou Wolff, Margaret Bardonner and Helen Kolling, members of the Allison Park Quiltmakers, stencil quilting lines onto a "Pinwheels" quilt. Allison Park, 1987.

social meaning and cultural cohesiveness. To explore this cultural process more fully, our exhibition includes not only crafts traditions that have been transmitted "unbroken" across generations but also those which have been interrupted and later revived or reconstituted. Both are types of traditional crafts.

"Craft and Community" emphasizes the interrelationships of the individual craftsworker with the historical craft tradition and the broader community context. Drawing from our statewide survey of traditional arts, we faced the difficult question of how to represent the range and complexity of the craft and cultural traditions we encountered.

The team of fieldworkers who participated in the Traditional Arts Survey gathered in Harrisburg in June 1986 to reflect on the craftsworkers we had met. We asked ourselves what were the common elements among our individual contacts. Through days of discussion, we realized that the common elements were patterns of cultural experience: the transmission of knowledge and skill, the interactions of craftsworkers among themselves and with community members, the transformation of raw materials and the adaptive use of available resources, patterns of continuity and change in craft traditions, and the relationship between physical objects and community values, beliefs, experience, and identity.

We decided an in-depth case study format would be the best vehicle to interpret these broad themes to the public, and from our fieldnotes we chose for the exhibition ten case studies of craftsworkers currently active in Pennsylvania. All incorporate and explore the relationship of three key elements—craftsworker, community, and tradition—though each case study balances these elements differently.

The first two case studies focus on individual craftsworkers: the transmission of the craft from generation to generation, and the range of technical skills which the craftsworker employs to produce a single object. The next three expand that focus to explore individual craftsworkers in their various community contexts: in relationship to other traditional artists, in small-group interaction organized around craft activity, and in providing vital services to a rural community. The final five studies shift towards a consideration of craft traditions at the level of the community, defined in regional, ethnic or religious terms. Within this last section, we explore the intermeshing of region, resources, and craft activity; craft as expression of values and beliefs in religious and ethnic communities; craft in association with religious ritual; the impact of acculturation on craft activities in an immigrant community; and cultural revival in relation to popularization and tourism.

The case studies and the opening sampler offer a taste of the active crafts traditions in Pennsylvania. Objects drawn from rural and urban settings in twenty-four Pennsylvania counties represent twenty-six ethnic, occupational, regional, and religious traditions: Afro-American, Amish, Anglo-American, anthracite coal-mining, Caribbean, Croatian, Dutch, French, Eastern Orthodox, English, Hmong, German, Irish, Lithuanian, logging, Mennonite, Jewish, Native American, Pennsylvania German, Puerto Rican, Polish, riverboat life, Romanian, Slovak, Swedish, and Ukrainian. "Craft and Community" includes the work of needleworkers and lace makers; weavers of rugs, baskets, and Christmas ornaments; blacksmiths and gunsmiths; woodcarvers and stonecarvers; miners, loggers, and riverboat men; calligraphers, painters, and egg decorators; leather, bead, and quill workers; musical instrument, furniture, and carriage makers; potters and paper cutters.

Traditional crafts thrive in Pennsylvania today because they are powerful expressions of community values. To be sure, the pressures confronting these community traditions are real. Established ethnic communities struggle both to preserve the traditional knowledge and skills of former generations and to find a new generation of apprentices to study with current master craftsworkers. New immigrants cope with learning new ways and a new language, not knowing how their own cultural traditions will con-

Below:
Bob Rock uses a grinder to shape and sharpen the butcher knives he makes from "retired" two-handled buck saws. Everett, 1988.

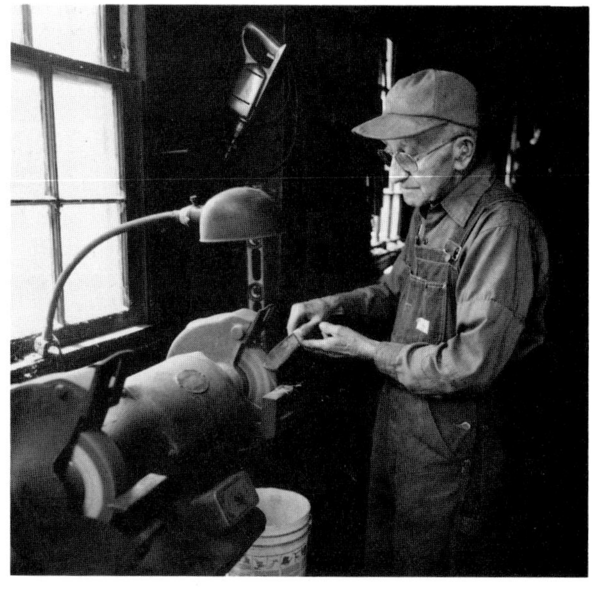

tribute to their present needs. Rural traditions, based on shared values of thrift and frugality on the farm, are threatened by ever-encroaching suburban development. Occupational skills are continually being replaced by new technologies, so that once vital knowledge and lore of the workplace is relegated to memory. Mass media promotes an American popular culture only distantly related to the real experiences of citizens.

The pressures exist, but the people are resilient and creatively respond to new situations. Craft traditions are adapted to meet changing times. The forms of the artifacts themselves may change. New tools and techniques may be employed, and new materials often substituted for old. The function of the artifact may also change, its value and meaning transformed. Artifacts, with their durability and tangible quality, may become a primary expression of community heritage.

Craftsworkers continue their efforts out of a desire and commitment to perpetuate their cultural traditions. Many sell their work, attempting to earn a living with the work of their hands, and yet they know that they cannot charge for the full investment of their time. Others would never sell their work; for these craftsworkers, it is a labor of love to be shared with family and close friends. Referring to an unassuming, yet intricately woven straw Christmas-tree ornament, one craftsworker commented to me, "You couldn't afford to buy it, and if you could, I wouldn't sell it."

Markets for traditional crafts are varied, with significant implications for the craftswork itself. Crafts continue to be produced for use within communities of shared values and beliefs. Musical instrument makers, whether their instrument is steel drum, *cuatro,* or *tamburitza,* are closely linked by shared knowledge, practice and aesthetic tradition with the musicians who purchase and play their instruments.

The rural blacksmith is vital in his community because his ability to creatively adapt used parts to solve mechanical problems is matched by his customer's traditional values, so foreign to our plastic, "throwaway" contemporary culture.

Yet increasingly, there is a demand for handcrafted artifacts across cultural boundaries, stimulated in part by media and advertising images of wholesome country living and exotic ethnic cultures. Urbanites purchase rustic hickory furniture and intricately stitched Hmong wall hangings. Tourists seek out Pennsylvania German quilts, hex signs, redware pottery, and *fraktur.* The travel industry is emerging as one of the most important forces shaping our economy and way of life; its impact is felt by many traditional craftsworkers who have to decide how to respond to this market. Tourists, weekend travelers, and visitors to crafts fairs and arts festivals all seek an experience that will transport them from their everyday world. When they come across a traditional craftsworker, they can take home tangible evidence of their "foreign" experience and vicariously relive their exposure to another place and time.[8]

Even when separated from their original social context, handcrafted artifacts continue to embody the image of that culture for outsiders, though that image may be only a pale reflection of the full range of values and meanings which are understood by cultural insiders. In the context of communities based on shared experience, the artifact, its maker, the aesthetic tradition it embodies, and the patterns of its use are among those elements which are interwoven to create the symbolic power of the handcrafted object. "Craft and Community" reaches beyond the popular images of rustic country life and exotic ethnic cultures to bring to wider public attention the vitality and creativity of traditional craftsmanship in contemporary society.

Notes

1. Beatrix T. Rumford, "Uncommon Art of the Common People: A Review of Trends in Collecting and Exhibiting of American Folk Art," in *Perspectives on American Folk Art*, eds. Ian Quimby and Scott Swank (New York: W. W. Norton, 1980), pp. 13-53.

2. Barre Toelken, "In the Stream of Life: An Essay on Oregon Folk Art." In *Webfoots and Bunchgrassers: Folk Art of the Oregon Country*, ed. Suzi Jones (Salem: Oregon Arts Commission, 1980), pp. 7-38.

3. Howard Becker, *Art Worlds* (Berkeley: University of California Press, 1982).

4. "Craft and Community" follows the lead established by previous exhibitions curated by folklorists in Oregon, Vermont, Idaho, Iowa and Wisconsin. See Suzi Jones, ed., *Webfoots and Bunchgrassers: Folk Art of the Oregon Country* (Salem: Oregon Arts Commission, 1980); Jane Beck, ed., *Always in Season: Folk Art and Traditional Culture in Vermont* (Montpelier, Vermont Council on the Arts, 1982); Steve Siporin, ed., *Folk Art of Idaho: "We came to where we were supposed to be"* (Boise: Idaho Commission on the Arts, 1984); Steve Ohrn, ed., *Passing Time and Traditions: Contemporary Iowa Folk Artists* (Ames: Iowa State University Press, 1984); and Robert Teske, ed., *From Hardanger to Harleys: A Survey of Wisconsin Folk Art* (Sheboygan: John Michael Kohler Arts Center, 1987). For an overview of developments in this field, see Robert Teske, "State Folk Art Exhibitions: Review and Preview," in *The Conservation of Culture: Folklorists and the Public Sector*, ed. Burt Feintuch (Lexington: University of Kentucky Press, 1988), pp. 109-17.

5. Henry Glassie, "The Idea of Folk Art," in *Folk Art and Art Worlds*, eds. John Vlach and Simon Bronner (Ann Arbor: UMI Research Press, 1986), pp. 269-74.

6. Charles Camp, " 'The Craft So Longe to Lerne': Traditional Craftsmanship and Its Uses in Contemporary Society," in *Traditional Craftsmanship in America: A Diagnostic Report*, ed. Charles Camp (Washington, D.C.: National Council for the Traditional Arts, 1983).

7. Dell Hymes, "Folklore's Nature and the Sun's Myth," *Journal of American Folklore* 88 (1975): 345-69.

8. Dean MacCannell writes, "For moderns, reality and authenticity are thought to be elsewhere: in other historical periods and other cultures, in purer, simpler lifestyles," in *The Tourist: A New Theory of the Leisure Class* (New York: Schocken Books, 1976), p. 3.

Suggested Reading

Appadurai, Arjun, ed. *The Social Life of Things: Commodities in Cultural Perspective,* Cambridge: Cambridge University Press, 1986.

Bronner, Simon, ed. *American Folk Art: A Guide to Sources.* New York: Garland Publishing, Inc., 1984.

__________. *American Material Culture and Folklife: A Prologue and Dialogue.* Ann Arbor: UMI Research Press, 1985.

Camp, Charles, ed. *Traditional Craftsmanship in America: A Diagnostic Report.* Washington, D.C.: National Council for the Traditional Arts, 1983.

Glassie, Henry. *Pattern in the Material Folk Culture of the Eastern United States.* Philadelphia: University of Pennsylvania, 1968.

Feintuch, Burt, ed. *The Conservation of Culture: Folklorists and the Public Sector.* Lexington: The University Press of Kentucky, 1988.

Graburn, Nelson H.H., ed. *Ethnic and Tourist Arts: Cultural Expressions from the Fourth World.* Berkeley: University of California Press, 1976.

Hall, Patricia and Charlie Seemann, eds. *Folklife and Museums: Selected Readings.* Nashville: American Association for State and Local History, 1987.

MacCannell, Dean. *The Tourist: A New Theory of the Leisure Class.* New York: Schocken Books, 1976.

Quimby, Ian M.G. and Scott T. Swank, eds. *Perspectives on American Folk Art.* New York: W. W. Norton, 1980.

Vlach, John Michael and Simon J. Bronner, eds. *Folk Art and Art Worlds.* Ann Arbor: UMI Research Press, 1986.

THE WOOD FAMILY:
Generations of Stone Carvers in Delaware County

J. Joseph Edgette

One of the most distinctive characteristics of traditional craftsmanship is the transmission of knowledge and skills from generation to generation. Younger artisans learn the techniques of their elders through apprenticeship, informal instruction, observation, imitation, and practice. In the process, innovation and adaptation in the form, function, or production techniques of traditionally crafted artifacts is as common as stability and continuity. The knowledge and skills learned as an apprentice can be highly adaptable, allowing a new generation to develop forms which depart from the past or to utilize techniques and technologies unavailable to the preceding generation of craftsworkers.

The Wood family of Delaware County, Pennsylvania offers an excellent example of both stability and adaptability as a particular craft, in this case stonecarving, has evolved over four generations. Since 1848 this family has excelled in producing carved gravestones used in the greater Philadelphia area, adapting their techniques to technological developments and providing stone memorials to meet the standards and preferences of succeeding generations.

Born in West Philadelphia in 1822 and reared there, Aaron Wood was a stonecutter who made marble steps, window sills, and lintels for the countless brick houses then being built in that part of the city. According to family history, Wood sometimes engaged in a system of barter for his work. For example, he received meat from local butchers in exchange for the marble cutting blocks he fashioned. To settle the debt of another transaction, a Bucks County man paid him with the deed to three acres of land, which remains in the Wood family to this day.[1]

Demand for Wood's craftsmanship was high in the pre-Civil War decades before steel began to replace stone in the construction trade. But later Wood had to adapt to changing times. At first, he cut and carved marble gravestones only infrequently, upon request from his more affluent customers who appreciated his skill in working stone. As his construction related work decreased, however, Wood recognized the potential in this new sideline. Philadelphia was growing rapidly, and the increasing population, and concomitantly the increasing number of deaths, led to greater demand for tombstones. Still, not all stonecutters were able to make the transition to carving as Aaron did because the carving added an additional artistic dimension to the work.

Grave markers have always reflected community attitudes towards death and dying. Indeed the carver's work becomes the lasting physical evidence of these cultural values. In some communities and in some periods plain, "undressed" grave markers lacking any adornment or carving, simply provide information about the deceased. During the 18th century, gravestone carvers would cut a tablet of stone and inscribe on it only the name and dates of birth and death of the person interred. Early in the 19th century gravemarkers commonly contained more information about the deceased, such as the occupation, cause of death, and societal affiliations. More detailed iconography also characterized this period.

Judging from the demand for his carvings, Aaron Wood was successful in meeting the more elaborate tastes and needs of his era's clients. Utilizing the technology of his day, he would draw a wire back and forth across a block of stone to cut a groove. He would next pour sand into the groove so that the friction of the wire and the sand would slowly cut the stone. Then, he would use a hand chisel and mallet to carve individual letters on the stone's face. When visual designs were requested, he would use various chisels and bush hammers. Though tedious and time consuming, these techniques produced works of fine craftsmanship. His block letters were both raised and carved in relief. His decorative carving typically incorporated free flowing lines and floral designs. In short, Aaron Wood's work reflects the deliberate and careful transformation of raw stone into a personalized memorial.

Aaron Wood was aware of varying religious preferences of the times and carved his markers accordingly. Gravestones for Catholics, for example, contained a cross or some other symbol associated with the Church: the letters "I H S" (derived from the Greek *Iesous Heneteros Soter*, meaning "Jesus our Savior"), a suitable Biblical quotation, or a visual or verbal reference to a saint or the Blessed Virgin. His grave markers for Protestants, on the other hand, often included scriptural passages and motifs representing resurrection or the virtues of faith, hope, and charity. Markers for Quakers and the "plain" sects, Amish and Mennonites, were appropriately simple.

In addition to these denominational preferences, Aaron Wood's diary entries and letters show that the development of public cemeteries brought additional rules and regulations. For example, guidelines limited the size of the marker and the extent to which iconography could be employed.

Above:
Formerly a flower shop opposite Fernwood Cemetery in Lansdowne, the H. C. Wood Art Memorials building has served as the office and display room since 1918. Lansdowne, 1918.

Below:
The introduction of automated tools in the 1940s enabled the stonecarver to more easily polish the finished stone. Lansdowne, c. 1948.

Having achieved a reputation as a gravestone carver and recognizing the need for his services, Aaron Wood established his business. The original shop was located on the front and side yards of his house, at the corner of Market and 33rd Streets in Philadelphia. By 1870 he had opened a branch of his company, which was run by his sons Thomas H. (1858-1929), J. Frank (1847-1920), and Harvard C. (1858-1937). Within twenty-five years these three brothers had purchased the business from their father. Eventually Harvard C. Wood took the leadership of the company as J. Frank sold his interest and Thomas died. In 1896 the company moved to its present location directly across from the main gate to Fernwood Cemetery, Upper Darby. The Woods have expanded and renovated their facilities four times in the last ninety-two years.

When the three brothers went into business, they continued their father's tradition of fine craftsmanship. Though generally similar in style to their father's work, the carvings of each of the sons varied in technique and attention to detail. Thomas' work was closer to actual sculpture than that of any of the others. He created numerous memorials with sculptural renderings, many of which remain in excellent condition. Harvard's work followed Victorian standards calling for elaborate motifs, great height, complex railings, and attractively carved monuments. Many examples of his work can be found in the Laurel Hill Cemetery in Philadelphia, one of the parklike burial grounds that opened in American cities during the Victorian era.[2]

Much of the innovation in this generation's work was due to the advancing technology of the day. Harvard Wood himself developed new sandblasting techniques, and pneumatic drills and bits slowly replaced mallets and chisels. As steam power made the work of the carver less tedious, it became possible to deal with mass. Such technology and the methods that developed along with it enabled the craftsworker to concentrate on greater detail in carving. Even the letters could be cut deeper into the stone, giving both a richer and more exacting quality.

Harvard Wood, Jr., came into the business in 1928 after completing training as a civil engineer. His work is contemporary in design and clearly reflects his own personal skill and style. His use of power tools, advanced sandblasting techniques, and granite instead of marble give Harvard Wood, Jr.'s memorials greater dimension and further detailing than those of his forebears.

In 1935, when Harvard Wood, Jr., became head of the company, he changed its name to the Steam Marble and Granite Works, advertising the introduction of steam power and the use of additional rock materials. With his engineering background, his progressive ideas, and his knowledge of memorials, he attempted to "restore memorial art to its ancient position as a spiritual and sociological factor in the evolution of civilization."[3] He not only revolutionized the marketing of gravestones by building a modern, glass-enclosed monument showroom, but he also designed the building for mechanized work. He introduced an electrically operated crane to move the stones and steam-power to run cutters, drills, sandblasters, and polishers. His adaptation of current technology transformed the work place and craft process; nevertheless, his work maintained a continuity of form, function, and craftsworker-customer interaction.

Harvard C. Wood III joined his father in the family enterprise in 1967. As did the three preceding generations of Wood family craftsmen, Harvard Wood III has adapted the latest technological advances in stone carving. Sandblasting techniques have continued to change, while stronger epoxies and more highly advanced cutting and carving tools, including lasers, offer the craftsworker a greater range of control in carving and thus a greater outlet for artistic expression. The gravestone carver now has the ability to combine the stone with various materials including ceramics, glass, plastic, plaster of paris, laminated wood, brick, and various metal alloys, either inlaid into the stone or attached to it with epoxies.

Harvard Wood III has access to the newest carving techniques and technology, and like the generations before him, he uses his resources to achieve greater flexibility for creative expression. Interestingly, Harvard's work has taken a conscious turn toward adapting old forms to present uses. To meet customer demand and his own sense of artistry, he has drawn from the repertoire of colonial New England gravestone art, a tradition quite outside his own family heritage. His use of slate instead of marble or granite is also consistent with this interest.

Below:
Harvard C. Wood, III, removes the rubber stencil used for sandblasting the design and lettering onto the stone. This latest technique has streamlined the carving process. Lansdowne, 1988.

One recent customer who ordered a stone for her parents felt that considering the age of the particular cemetery and her parents' interest in antiques, it would be inappropriate to use a modern stone.[4] In consultation with Harvard Wood III, the customer decided to match the existing gravestones in St. David's Church yard. Customer and carver jointly agreed to a grave marker based on the colonial style, even to the point of adopting the old lettering. Research on the lettering alone took Harvard several weeks. Additional research led to other design features of the gravestone, including the use of the wife's full maiden name, a customary practice of the period. The granite for the stone was quarried in Westerly, R.I., a little village with great sentimental attachment for the family. Despite the intended visual similarities to the seventeenth-century forms, this 1985 gravestone was not a mere period replica. For example, the wording conveyed a contemporary sensibility of equal treatment for husband and wife, rather than the earlier convention in which the wife was given lesser attention.

Over the generations thousands of markers have been carved in the Wood family business, but not every stone was carved by a Wood. As many as twenty men worked in the Wood monument shop at a given time, learning the craft from one of the Wood generations and later earning their livelihood by carving grave markers. Today the traditional gravestone carver is a rare breed, facing competition from companies employing automated, even computerized, mass-production techniques.

Left:
Carved by Harvard C. Wood, III, in 1987 for the parents of Mrs. H. Edward Rothe, this marker was designed to replicate the lettering, motifs and shape of colonial markers. St. David's Episcopal Churchyard, Wayne, 1988.

Below:
Though techniques have changed since this 1930 interior view of the H. C. Wood Shop, today's shop is just as crowded with stones in various stages of carving. Lansdowne, c. 1930.

Although the Wood family has taken advantage of available technological advances in each generation, the carvers have never lost sight of the individual stone as memorial to the deceased. The client-carver relationship has also changed little over four generations. Business records document that each job interaction has proceeded along similar lines. Through direct consultation, the carver personally addresses the client's needs and design interests. The carver then prepares a sketch from which the rendering is made. The client must approve the visual rendering, at which point the carver proceeds to prepare the stone and later erect it at the grave site. By offering expert counsel, the Wood family has consistently produced gravestones that are socially appropriate, acceptable to the client, and aesthetically pleasing.

Techniques have indeed changed over four generations from Aaron Wood to Harvard C. Wood III. Yet, basic elements of form and design have remained constant, as has the attention given to the details of carving stones individually. By incorporating the client's values in the monument, the stonecarver plays a key role in revealing familial, religious, and broader social attitudes towards death and bereavement. The Wood family demonstrates the ways a traditional craft adapts to changing times. Each generation has clearly passed on to the next its dedication to this craft. In turn, each new generation has built on its inheritance, maintaining traditional values of craftsmanship and community while seeking new techniques and modes of expression.

Left:
Carved in 1910 with the Hebrew mnemonic for "May his soul be bound in life eternal," this marker illustrates the diverse clientele of the Wood family carvers. Springfield, 1988.

Sketch of funeral memorial
by Harvard C. Wood, Jr.
(checklist #22)

Notes

1. Interview with Harvard C. Wood, Jr., 1981.

2. Established in 1836, Laurel Hill Cemetery is the second oldest garden type, or "rural" cemetery in the United States.

3. Quoted from publicity material prepared for an interview of Harvard Wood, Jr. for a local newspaper, ca. 1953.

4. Based on an interview with Mrs. H. Edward Rothe on the day she inspected the completed grave marker prior to placement in the cemetery, March 1985.

Suggested Reading

Duval, F. and I. Rigby. *Early American Gravestone Art in Photographs*. New York: Dover, 1978.

Edgette, J. Joseph. "The Wood Family of Philadelphia: Four Generations of Stonecarving." In *By Land and By Sea: Studies in the Folklore of Work and Leisure*, edited by Roger Abrahams. Hatboro, Pa.: Legacy Books, 1985.

Forbes, Harriette M. *Gravestones of Early New England and the Men Who Made Them*. Princeton: Pyne Press, 1955.

McDonald, Frank E. "Pennsylvania German Tombstone Art of Lebanon County, Pennsylvania." *Pennsylvania Folklife* 25, no. 1 (1976):2-19.

ROBERT MOORE:
Native American Craftsman

Thomas E. Graves

Is the deerhide correctly worked and softened? Are the beads the right size and color for the design and time period? Does the design correctly represent the tribe from which it is drawn? Are the beads being attached with the proper stitch? These are the questions Bob Moore is constantly asking, the concerns which form the basis for his skills. Technical considerations follow. Is this the correct technique to achieve the desired result? Is the process the correct one to create an aesthetically pleasing, authentic piece of Native American beadwork? The proper application of skills, as well as the proper use of hand tools, leads to a well-constructed article.

Bob Moore, who was born in 1929, is a Cherokee craftsman living in Boalsburg, Centre County, Pennsylvania. He practices traditional styles of Native American tanning, leatherwork, and decoration with quills, and wampum and glass beads. Although his father practiced Native American wood sculpting, his original interest in Native American crafts came from the Boy Scouts. From those early craft projects, his interest continued to grow. As his skills developed, he learned more about tribal differences in techniques and design. Having practiced Native American crafts as a hobby most of his life, he quit his job in 1980 to devote his full efforts to produce objects for sale. Moore now works out of a combined workshop and retail store near his home in Boalsburg and maintains another shop in his house.

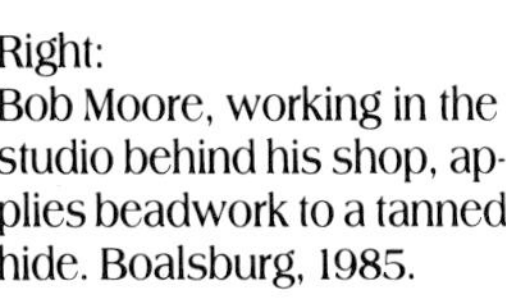

Right:
Bob Moore, working in the studio behind his shop, applies beadwork to a tanned hide. Boalsburg, 1985.

In creating an object, Moore generally goes through several stages, including preparation of the hide, layout of the project, decoration, and final assembly. Rather than using commercially prepared and tanned hides, Moore takes pride in preparing hides himself, and tanning them with deer brains and smoke. The result is a much softer and more usable hide than he can otherwise obtain. Observers have noted the softness and good condition of century-old, native-tanned leather, and some doubt that contemporary, commercially tanned leather will fare as well. One of his neighbors hunts deer and saves the hides for him, and some customers will bring him hides from their catch. Although Moore used to hunt with a bow, for the last several years he just has not had the time so he is dependent on others for his hides. He primarily works with deerhide, but he has also worked with hides from moose and elk.

Right top:
After stretching the hide on a frame, Bob Moore uses a scraper he made from a deer antler and metal blade to remove the outside hair and the inside membrane. Boalsburg, 1987.

Right center: The brains of the animal are cooked over a low fire and brushed into both sides of the hide to strengthen and soften it. Boalsburg, 1987.

Right bottom:
Once the hide has dried, Bob Moore removes it from the frame and stretches it to make it soft and pliable. Boalsburg, 1987.

The preparation of the hide is the most tedious part of his work as all the flesh and membranes must be scraped off. The inner membrane is removed first while the hide is draped over a log which acts as a combination form and worktable. The hide is then stretched on a frame and each side is scraped to remove all the membranes and hair. Heated deer brain is worked into the stretched hide. Once he has cured the hide through the "braining" process, Moore pokes the stretched hide with a canoe paddle to make it pliable. He next removes the hide from the stretcher and works it by hand, pulling, twisting, and knotting the hide to make it soft. Finally, the hide is wrapped over a rope and worked back and forth. By now the hide is soft and pliable and may be used for clothing and other artifacts. For preservation and coloring, Moore usually will smoke the hide by hanging it over a smoldering fire tied or sewn together with as many other hides as are ready. Optimally the fire is smoldering with a lot of smoke but no flames. Stakes are used to prop open the bottom of the hides in a tent shape. The hides have to be reversed and sometimes turned inside out to make sure they are thoroughly smoked. The longer the hides are smoked, the darker will be the finished product. Before he completes this work, Moore cuts off a corner of the hide and places it on the fire as a sacrifice to thank and honor the deer's spirit.

Moore makes his own scrapers and stretchers. He explains that pre-contact tools would have had stone, obsidian, or bone surfaces, but he is quick to point out that Native Americans readily adopted new tools after their contact with the Europeans. His scrapers do have metal blades. The preliminary working of the hide with a canoe paddle is Moore's own idea. This step helps stretch the fibers and lessens the need for working by hand. Although there are now booklets available that describe how to brain tan deer-

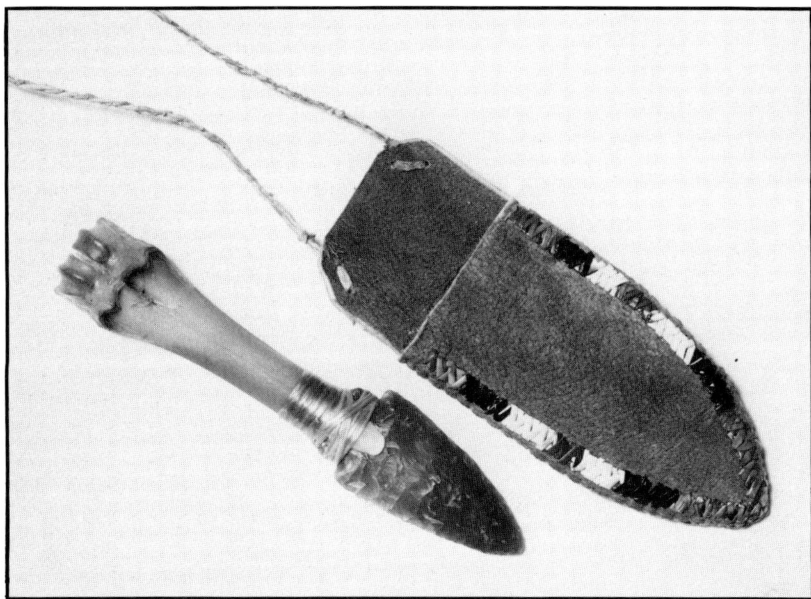

hide, there were none when he started to teach himself this process about fifteen years ago. It took him five years before he thought the result started to "look right" and another five years before he was satisfied with the result. He still continually refines his technique.

When the hides are ready, they can be used for clothing, moccasins, bags, knife sheaths, or any number of other objects (see Color Plates #4 and 5). Once he decides what he wants to make, Moore determines what tribe and time period he wants to represent. This decision will affect the final design and appearance of the object. Will the object require quillwork or beads? If beads, what size beads? Which designs and colors are suitable? What is an appropriate shape for the artifact and how should it be put together? These concerns are important for him and for many of his customers. Native Americans are made up of many culturally diverse groups, each with its own set of preferred designs, colors, and styles. Moore feels it is only right to adhere to, and, therefore honor these traditions and to recognize the role of history. Authentic wampum, he says, are made from the quahog shell with the shell's natural colors of white or purple; they should be dyed in natural vegetable colors. Yet over time styles have changed, especially after materials became available from the Europeans. For example, the earliest beads were large; smaller beads became available later.

Many of his customers are collectors and "users" of Native American crafts and know what they want. The collectors may be Native American themselves and want to collect pieces reflecting their own specific culture. The users might be Native Americans or they might be "Black Powder" enthusiasts who want to re-create the frontier experience. Thus he may get a request for Iroquois moccasins in the style of the 1820s or for a complete set of pre-contact Lenni Lenape work clothes. Occasionally, he is requested to duplicate a museum piece. Beyond the souvenir hunters who wander into his shop, Moore has an educated clientele who would know if he were not being true to tribal styles. Between his personal satisfaction and his customer's desires, he is doubly motivated to authentically create, or re-create, Native American articles.

Moore decries "generic Indian beadwork" which is suggestive of Native American designs but have no real tribal affiliation. Additionally, he says, many of these generic pieces are poorly constructed and give Native American crafts a bad reputation. He admits that not all of the inexpensive and poorly made Indian souvenirs are made by outsiders. Several Native American craftspeople in the Southwest over the last several decades, for example, have found it more expedient to make salable items that are small, inexpensive, and look like Indian art rather than produce works of quality from their own cultural heritage. Although Moore does make inexpensive items for the souvenir hunter or tourist who visits his shop, these items authentically represent specific tribal traditions.

Many of the craftspeople in the Southwest who make objects specifically for sale to outsiders have worked under the influence of the art establishment; collectors and sellers have told these artisans what they want. Since the end of the last century this process has led to a mix between the traditional forms, what the craftspeople think their customers want, and what the collectors think "Indian" things should look like.

Moore also feels outside influences, including the Black Powder enthusiasts and Native American collectors, but these influences drive him toward continued research into historically accurate designs. He maintains his own research library and enjoys the experience of examining items when collectors bring in their acquisitions to show him. His library research and his examination of extant pieces help him in the design of his own work. He is not, however, a copy artist. He prefers to determine the correct style, designs, and colors and then to work within that tradition, to make something new rather than to copy another item. He will make a copy of something only when a customer specifically requests one.

After preparing the hides, Moore cuts carefully sized pieces and adds the decoration. He has the kind of decoration he wants in his mind as he selects the proper size and color beads, lays them out on a work tray he made for himself, and sets to work. No design is drawn, graphed, or marked onto the leather: to do so would not be authentic. The placing of the design is done completely by eye. The first bead is placed on the leather and the design grows from that point. In sewing quills, or glass or wampum beads he is careful that the needle does not go all the way through the leather. Rather it is "tunneled" into the leather. If the thread did show on the reverse side of a piece of clothing, for instance, it would rub against the skin and be uncomfortable. Also, the exposed thread would wear and eventually break, causing the ruin of the design. He finds the brain-tanned hide better suited for his sewing technique because commercially tanned hides still have some of the "grain" (skin) on them and if the thread is passed through only the grain layer, it may cause the grain to pull away from the rest of the leather.

Of the three materials used to form the decorations, Moore prepares only porcupine quills himself. He usually purchases the quills but dyes them himself using dyes from local plants. If a customer wants some quillwork requiring a color derived from a plant not in season, he will use chemical dyes for that specific order. He purchases ready-made wampum beads from the Iroquois. Although he has made his own in the past, shaping and drilling the quahog shells just takes more time than he has to put into making wampum. His glass beads are factory-made in Czechoslovakia.

Moore knows how to make "thread" from sinew, and he does use sinew when he feels it is needed. Routinely, though, he uses modern thread for his beadwork. He uses long pieces from a large spool to sew the beads onto the leather. A long thread may seem awkward to work with, but the beadwork will be stronger the fewer times he has to add new pieces of thread. The final knot is buried into the beadwork so that it cannot be seen. One slipped knot can destroy several hours' work as Moore spends an average of one hour for one square inch of beadwork.

When appropriate, Moore uses a hand loom to make belts, sweat bands, and other objects. Hand loom projects, however, are commonly used as introductions to Native American beadwork and promote the generic designs which Moore dislikes as not being authentic.

Although Moore will produce articles from almost any of the tribal regions of North America, he says that most of what he makes comes from the Eastern Woodlands cultures. He is committed to preserving the traditions of the Eastern Woodlands tribes, as these are not as well known as other tribal traditions and historically were almost eliminated. The tribes he favors include those Algonkian and Iroquoian-speaking tribes that originally inhabited Pennsylvania, such as the Lenni Lenape (also known as the Delaware) and the Susquehanna (also known as the Conestoga) and neighboring tribes such as the Erie and the Iroquois "Five Nations"—the Seneca, Cayuga, Oneida, Onondaga, and Mohawk. Some of these tribes lived as far as Maine and Canada to the north, Virginia to the south, and the Mississippi to the west, for boundaries were nonexistent. The Five Nations and the Erie, for example, also had footholds in Pennsylvania, and the Lenni Lenape lived in New Jersey and Delaware as well as Pennsylvania.

Moore, himself, is Cherokee. The Cherokee originally lived in what is now the western Carolinas and eastern Tennessee. In the 1830s a

Right:
Ceremonial fan by Robert C. Moore (checklist #50)

large portion was forcibly relocated to present-day Oklahoma and became known as the Western Band of Cherokees. The several thousand who remained behind in their ancestral areas became known as the Eastern Band of Cherokees. Some family groups from the Eastern Band moved northward along the Appalachian Mountains, against the southern stream of Pennsylvania Germans and Scotch-Irish, into Pennsylvania. Moore's father's family arrived in central Pennsylvania as part of this northern migration in the 1830s. Centre County does not have a large or organized resident population of Native Americans. Moore thus works in relative ethnic seclusion except for a large transient population of Native Americans enrolled in the Native American Leadership Program at nearby Pennsylvania State University who often will seek him out.

Through his skills and through his learning, Bob Moore strives to produce authentically made and decorated Native American objects. He is always learning more about various cultural design traditions, and he is constantly educating his customers about the value and importance of authentic work. In his roles as craftsperson and educator he has taken on apprentices through the Apprenticeship in Traditional Arts Program administered by the Pennsylvania Council on the Arts and the Pennsylvania Heritage Affairs Commission. His apprentices have all, by chance, had Eastern Woodlands affiliations, but their knowledge of native culture has differed widely, from that of the Cherokee apprentice who knew more about the Plains and Southwestern cultures because of where he grew up to that of the Ojibwa apprentice who had moved away from her people and had not learned the traditional lore her family still feels is important. He teaches the culture as well as his skills, for the two cannot be divorced.

Bob Moore continually seeks to increase his repertoire of designs and to improve and refine the skills he uses to execute them. His range of skills is vitally important to his work, but he aims beyond technical excellence. His prime concern is the cultural authenticity of his work.

Suggested Reading

American Indian Art Magazine

Coe, Ralph T. *Lost and Found Traditions: Native American Art, 1965-1985.* New York: American Federation of Arts, 1986.

Belitz, Larry. *Brain-Tanning the Sioux Way.* Hot Springs, S.D.: by the author, 1973.

Introduction to American Indian Art (2 vols.). New York: The Exposition of Indian Tribal Arts, Inc., 1931.

Miles, Charles. *Indian & Eskimo Artifacts of North America.* New York: Bonanza, 1963.

Newcomb, William W., Jr. *North American Indians: An Anthropological Perspective.* Santa Monica: Goodyear Publishing Company, 1974.

TERRENCE CAMERON AND AGUEDO BELTRAN:
Musical Instrument Makers

John Reynolds

The performance of traditional music in ethnic communities can be a powerful cultural expression. The realization of this expression often depends upon the skills of individual instrument makers, since many traditional instruments are not mass produced. The makers of traditional instruments fill a unique role by practicing one specialized activity, craft, to support another, music making. Our two examples, a maker of steel "pans" and a *cuatro* maker, provide instruments rarely available in the mass marketplace. Both craftsmen have adapted to the American urban environment. Both receive orders for instruments through an informal network of performers, and neither does any advertising.

In a small West Philadelphia row-house basement, Terrence Cameron turns common 55-gallon oil drums into high quality musical instruments. Cameron builds steel pans, the Caribbean instruments used in steel bands. His workshop is not fancy: a bare electric light bulb hangs from the ceiling, the walls are unfinished, and scattered around are drums in various stages of development. His tools are quite modest: chisels, a compass, a small electric saw, a butane torch, hammers, and a set of homemade patterns. In the corner is a finished set of tenor pans, well worn with years of use. Cameron is a quiet personable man, patient and determined; he is also a fine performer.

Born on the island of Grenada in 1941, Cameron had moved with his family to Trinidad by the mid-forties. From his early childhood he vividly remembers hearing The Starlight Syncopators, a steel band in San Juan, Trinidad. In 1956, much to the trepidation of his parents, he joined a steel band called The Bell Boys and learned to play the double tenors, the prime melodic pan set in an orchestra. "My parents were opposed to my involvement with the band. Steel bands had the reputation of being a rough crowd."[1] Indeed, in the forties and fifties membership signified rejection of the norms of society and ruling class values.

Steel bands evolved from *tamboo bamboo* bands, which utilized various sized struck bamboo lengths and were formed in the late nineteenth century as a reaction against an official ban on African drumming. The tamboo bamboo bands persisted until the late forties and augmented the bamboo with other naturally resonant articles such as tin boxes, bottles, bits of iron, and dustpans. Spree Simon is credited with tuning a tin dustpan to one or more pitches. As legend goes, he subsequently turned to 55-gallon oil drums abundant from World War II and the discovery of oil on the islands because of their thicker and more stable metal.[2] Instruments made from the oil drums soon developed into various classes (tenor pans, guitar pans, cello pans, and bass pans) covering the entire musical range from bass to soprano. Fierce competition between rival bands fostered gang fights as well as innovation in both tuning and design techniques. Gradually steel bands were accepted into mainstream society, and band rivalries were channelled into steel drum competitions. Although the early bands played primarily dance music, the intensity of the competitions quickly produced a more sophisticated concert repertoire.[3]

Above:
Terrence Cameron uses a mallet to shape the concave surface of the pan drum. This is called "flashing the pan." Philadelphia, 1986.

The repertoire performed by these bands include the best known music of the islands: calypso dance forms. Calypso, which blends African, Hispanic, British, and French elements, quickly spread throughout the Caribbean and remains popular today. Its history is closely tied to the celebration of Carnival in the Port of Spain, with elaborate costuming and parades. The use of song for topical and social satire is a distinctive feature of calypso.

A more modern development is the performance of western classical music by the bands in organized competitions. Marches, opera overtures, and symphonic movements are all performed by large and well-rehearsed bands. Like a western orchestra, a steel drum band has "sections" corresponding to the strings, the brass, the woodwinds, and so on. Learning and performing this orchestral style is a challenge for the drummers, considering that notation systems for the steel drum orchestra have only recently been developed.

At the age of 17 Cameron joined the Rhapsody Steel Orchestra led by Stanley Warner, who taught him how to construct steel pans. "Pan makers would travel to their customers' homes and stay while they would make the drum set." Through the social network of these competition bands, the steel pan makers obtained work and grew more sophisticated as did the pans they produced. The best makers became professionals with established shops. In 1963 Cameron formed the Sonnets, his first band. He made the entire drum set for the band. "I had to get a little assistance from Mr. Warner in the final tuning." During the next two or three years Cameron played with his band and established a reputation as a maker but eventually received so many orders for drums that he left the band, traveling to Tobago, Barbados, and other islands in the West Indies as a full time maker.

Seven years later, Cameron joined the Trinidad Cotellio All Stars, a top band in Trinidad, and traveled to New York City. After the tour Cameron decided to stay in the United States, and he moved to Philadelphia in 1979. "When I was in bands, I got a lot of work," he recalls. Interspersed with pan making were jobs in building construction. Cameron established his contacts for further pan making through the informal network of musicians up and down the East Coast. He now receives many orders from New York City, which has the nation's highest concentration of Trinidadians.[4]

The "color" of any instrument is determined by the composition of the construction materials, the method that produces the vibrating air, and the number of the simultaneous vibrational areas available. The components of the steel drum family are tuned chromatic idiophones. Other members of this family of instruments constructed of inherently resonant materials includes the xylophone and marimba. Vibrating areas are struck to produce distinct and stable pitches, and since more than one note may be played simultaneously, contrapuntal and harmonic music may be performed. Steel drums are unlike other struck idiophones, however, because (especially in the higher-pitched drums) many of the vibrating areas are contiguous on a common surface. These many sound areas on the common tables vibrate sympathetically to produce complex wave forms which are reinforced by the empty sound chamber.

Modern steel pans are made in sets of four, three, or two. Bass pans (or "tuned booms"), in sets of two to four drums, cover a small range of two to five notes. Sets of three drums (called cello pans) and double or treble guitar pans, double seconds, and sets of two tenor pans cover the alto to soprano ranges chromatically.

The construction of a steel drum involves a number of different skills. The maker must have excellent control over basic metal working tools, a fundamental understanding of the physics of music, and an excellent ear. A compass to lay out radii, a hammer to sink the pan, a set of patterns corresponding to the various notes, punches and metal chisels to groove the impressions, an electric metal saw to cut the drums, and a propane torch to temper the drum are the tools of the pan maker's trade. Traditional makers in Trinidad often use simple high temperature fires instead of the torch, and a hand saw rather than an electric saw to shorten the length of the higher-pitched drums.

The process starts with the selection of a suitable 55-gallon drum, ideally one of 20-18-gauge steel. The maker cuts off the top of the drum, then flips it over. He begins to sink or "flash" the pan by striking the former drum bottom from the outer rim to the center, creating a consistent concave surface extending down into the drum. This is one of the most critical points in drum-making because if the surface splits, the drum becomes unuseable.

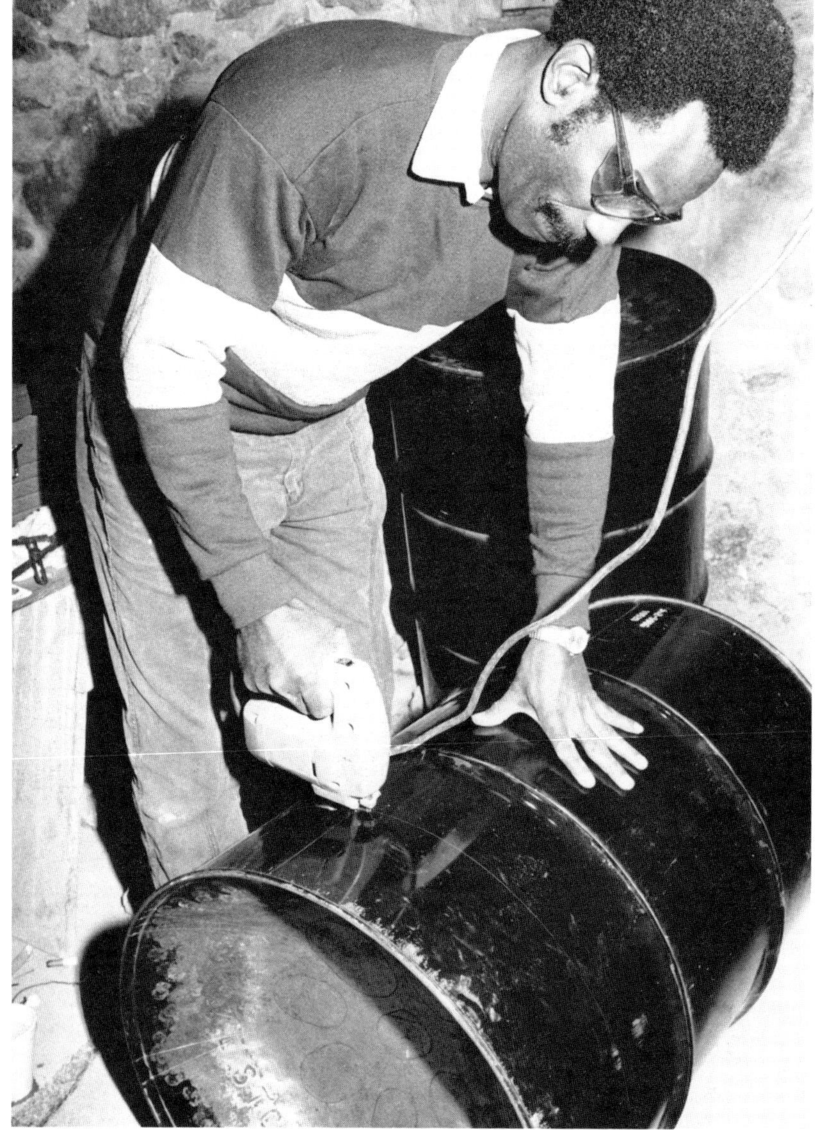

Below:
Once the surface has been shaped, the pan drum is separated from the remainder of the large steel drum. The larger the drum, the deeper the sound. Philadelphia, 1986.

The notes are laid out after the successful sinking of the pan. Depending on the musical range of the pan, notes are drawn upon the pan by means of unique patterns. Higher-pitched pans contain a greater number of notes than the lower-pitched pans. The relative size of the notes corresponds to the ratios of the harmonic sequence (the same ratios that dictate length of the strings in a piano). For example, bass pans may have as few as two or three notes, but double seconds or double tenors, which are sets of two drums, will cover two to three octaves (24 to 36 notes) with twelve to eighteen notes per pan. The lower range of the bass pans (60 to 90 hertz or vibrations per second) necessitates a vibrational surface of over 144 square inches to resonate so slowly. As the maker sequentially creates each higher pitch, smaller surfaces are required. The top range of the instrument requires vibrating areas as small as 1 to 2 square inches. Each area must be tuned to resonate at the proper musical frequency. To achieve this, radii are scribed on the top surface (originally the bottom of the drum) with a compass. The outer edges of these note patterns are grooved with a hammer and punch or metal chisel to insulate the vibrating surfaces with a ridge. The vibrating areas are then pounded into a slight convex pattern from underneath the drum, a step called "ponging up."[5] A rough tuning to bring the areas near the appropriate frequency also is done at this time.

The drums are heat treated to temper the steel. This is necessary to insure the integrity and longevity of the surfaces, and it further enhances the resonant properties of the drum by hardening the metal. The drums are heated red hot and then rapidly cooled by immersion in cold water. After tempering, the final tuning begins. Many contemporary makers use an electronic tuning device to bring the pitch of each area to the proper frequency. Adjusting

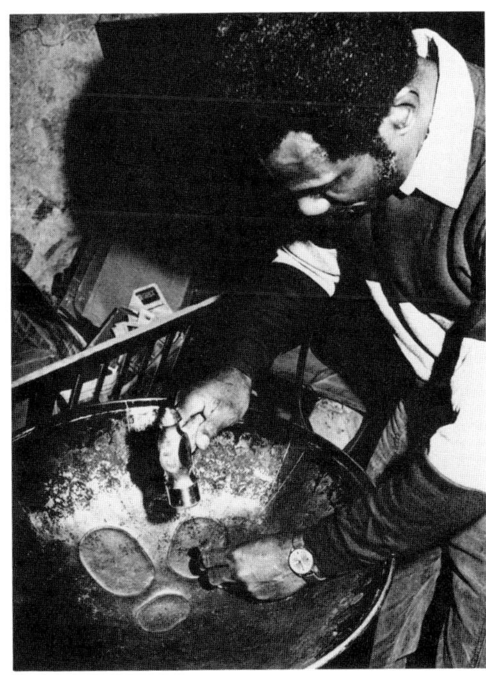

Left:
With a chisel, Terrence Cameron grooves the impressions on the drum to isolate the resonating areas. Philadelphia, 1986.

Below:
Various tools and stencils of the pan drummaker's trade. Philadelphia, 1986.

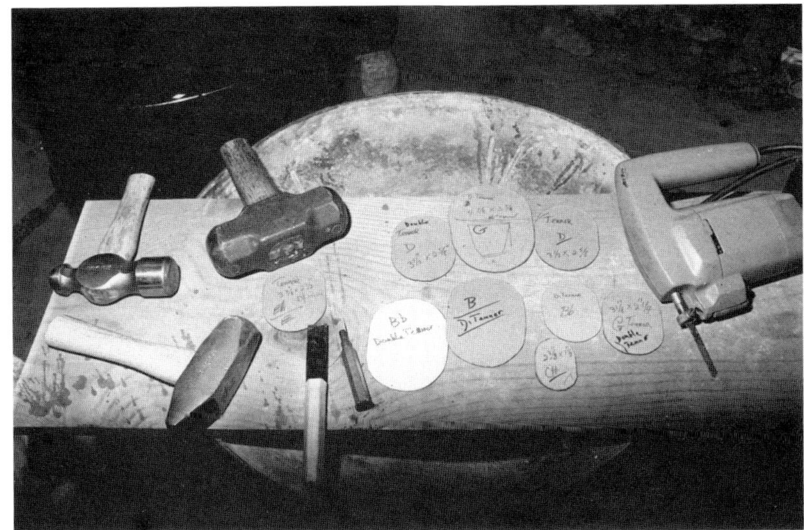

the tuning areas to a slightly more convex position raises the pitch; a more concave position lowers it. However, the final tuning is more complex than just adjusting each pitch to a "perfect" fixed frequency. The best makers of steel pans tune their pans like pianos by the well-tempered process (not to be confused with the heat treatment). This process of tuning a harmonic instrument "slightly out of tune" dates back to the time of Bach. It requires that the intervals (the frequency ratio between notes) be adjusted slightly to less than theoretical perfection so that the instrument can be played in all keys. In other words, the notes F# and Gb have identical frequencies in a well-tempered system although theoretically they have slightly different resonant frequencies. The net result of well-tempered tuning is equidistant half-tone intervals. Like piano tuners, pan makers must do the final tuning by ear. At the end of this process, some makers chrome plate their instruments for decorative and tonal effects.

In addition to his role as instrument maker, Cameron is a highly skilled player. Performance opportunities on the East Coast are very different from those in Trinidad and Tobago, where steel bands are in demand for social, ceremonial, and cultural performances. Considering that the majority of his work does not come from the Trinidadian community, Cameron has had to be flexible. To be sure, there are community dances, weddings, and the large Carnival celebration in New York; however, he performs in many other settings such as university functions, concerts for area arts institutions, casinos, and private parties outside the Caribbean community.

Because there are few skilled players on the East Coast, Cameron has had to act as teacher for a number of musicians. He also acts as arranger for his bands, teaching the musicians all the complex parts. As

Above:
Terrence Cameron with two pans, showing the top and side of the completed drums. Philadelphia, 1986.

a result of his high visibility as a musician and teacher, Cameron receives many orders from Boston, New York, Baltimore, and Washington to make new drums or to re-tune drums that have been damaged or have gone out of tune from metal fatigue. His visibility as an important and well-respected member of the Caribbean music community is critical for drum orders and performance dates. Cameron nearly supports himself from his instrumental work and only occasionally takes jobs in building construction to augment his income. Since steel band music has filtered into popular culture, Cameron's musical career has become even more significant.

Our second musical instrument maker to consider is North Philadelphia resident Aguedo Beltran. In his small, cramped, upstairs workroom he bends, cuts, and molds wood to make the *cuatro*, a plucked lute of the guitar family (see Color Plate #6). He patiently glues braces to the back of the top and speaks of his love for this instrument and the music played upon it. He is articulate and passionate about his work. He loves wooden instruments.

Aguedo Beltran was born in San Juan, Puerto Rico. Some of his earliest memories are of musicians performing traditional music for dances and other community functions. His father had a grocery business in Puerto Rico, but his uncles and other relatives were woodworkers. At the age of seven, Beltran and his family moved to New York. He attended school in the Bronx and studied auto mechanics and woodworking. "I loved the look and feel of musical instruments. I used to visit pawn shops as a teenager to see them, especially Spanish guitars. A Spanish guitar is a living soul. To a musician an instrument is a companion."[6]

Beltran started making cuatros for a number of reasons. As a boy in Puerto Rico, he played this instrument at Christmas time to accompany the *aguinaldo*, a repertory of well known folk and popular religious songs of Spanish derivation whose texts deal with the Christmas cycle.[7] Beltran is proud that the cuatro is native to Puerto Rico. Making these instruments reinforces his pride. "Not many young people are playing the cuatro. I see my culture disappearing and I just say no!"

The cuatro evolved from the Spanish *vihuela*. It has five double-course strings tuned in fourths. Until the late 19th century it had only four sets of strings. It is played with a plectrum, as is a guitar. The cuatro is capable of playing as the melodic lead or as a chordal rhythm instrument in an ensemble that might include other plucked instruments such as guitar, *tiple*, another four stringed instrument, and *tres*, a three stringed instrument. These ensembles might also include horns and various percussion instruments. Among the music performed on the cuatro are the forms of *bomba*, which include many dances of African origin such as *barmule*, *belen*, *candungo*. Also closely associated with the cuatro is the song genre known as *plena*. These songs frequently have topical themes expressed in a call and response structure with stanzas and refrains.[8] The cuatro is played much like the European and American mandolin. A singing tone is created by means of the *tremolo*, a rapid reiterating stroke of the plectrum over double-strung strings. Chords of all types and forms may be performed on the cuatro. The tuning is quite similar to the guitar, consequently many players double on that instrument.

Below:
Aguedo Beltran at his work bench with a partially completed Puerto Rican *cuatro*. The curved sides of the instrument are held in place by a series of clamps over a wooden mold. Philadelphia, 1986.

Beltran began to construct these instruments by sketching them from models. "I did not copy them exactly but adapted the designs." In visits to Puerto Rico he examined many instruments including those by Christobo Santiago, a leading instrument maker. In 1977 after making his fifth cuatro, Beltran met Rafael Hernandes in Philadelphia. From Hernandes he learned how to heat wood for bending sides and how to feel the density and stiffness of wood. Hernandes also taught Beltran about oil varnish, which he made from boiled linseed oil, colored dye, turpentine, and japan drier. Beltran also learned to apply French polish, the finish used on the necks of fine guitars, cuatros, and violins, which is made from shellac flakes.

From visits to makers in Puerto Rico Beltran gained more knowledge and learned other techniques. "In Puerto Rico the wood for cuatros must be cut during the full moon, for the wood is drier at this time. Otherwise it may rot." Also, he learned about the traditional glues made from the panapen tree. The tree yields a white latex which forms a powerful glue when dried in the sun. He now constructs his own molds and jigs to insure a consistent quality.

Having made nearly twenty cuatros in the past fifteen years, Beltran is well known among Puerto Rican traditional musicians in Philadelphia. Most of his instruments are used by East Coast musicians; however, a few are used by musicians in Puerto Rico. Like Cameron, he receives his orders through an informal network of musicians.

In Puerto Rico the cuatro is made from native woods. The soundboard is traditionally constructed from *grajumo*, a soft stringy wood found in the Caribbean islands. In its place Beltran substitutes either Canadian sitka spruce or in more expensive instruments, German spruce. For the back and sides, which usually are made from *guaragua* (guad-a-gwow), he uses Honduran mahogany or American black walnut. For the fingerboard, African ebony, Mexican rosewood, or East Indian rosewood replaces the customary *roble*. Typically cuatros have very little decoration around the central sound hole, perhaps just a single or double ring to reinforce the top. Beltran inlays fine rosettes imported from Spain which have intricate marquetry, and occasionally, he inlays abalone shell in the sound board.

These two remarkable men share a lot in common; both men have a deep commitment to their craft and their respective cultures. Beltran has shown resourcefulness in wood substitutions and his original approach to construction techniques. Cameron has readily adapted to the performance opportunities of the Philadelphia environment and proven to be a fine teacher and arranger. Both men are central to the perpetuation of their communities' traditional musics. The performers depend upon these craftsworkers to provide new instruments and to repair and adjust their old instruments. These craftsmen are an important source of knowledge for performing musicians, since many of their customers may be outside of the community at large. Their influence extends outside the community, many times across national boundaries. Both men's work is of very high quality. The personal service they provide to musicians is not generally available in the mass market for musical instruments, and the instruments they construct are powerful symbols of cultural pride and identity.

Notes

1. Interview with Terrence Cameron, Philadelphia, February, 1986.

2. John Bartholomew, *The Steel Band* (Oxford: Oxford University Press, 1980), p. 17.

3. Helen Meyers, "Trinidad and Tobago," in *The New Grove Dictionary of Music and Musicians*, edited by Stanlie Sadie (London: Macmillan Publishers, Ltd., 1980), Vol. 19, p. 149.

4. Roy S. Bryce-Laporte and Delores M. Mortimer, editors, *Caribbean Immigration to the United States* (Washington D.C.: Research Institute on Immigration and Ethnic Studies, Smithsonian Institution, 1983), p. 48.

5. Bartholomew, *The Steel Band*, p. 33.

6. Interview with Aguedo Beltran, Philadelphia, July, 1986.

7. Donald Thompson, "Puerto Rico," in *The New Grove Dictionary*, Vol. 15, p. 443.

8. Ibid., p. 444.

Suggested Reading

Bartholomew, John. *The Steel Band*. Oxford: Oxford University Press, 1980.

Dominguez, Virginia R. *From Neighbor to Stranger: The Dilemma of the Caribbean Peoples in the United States*. New Haven: Yale University Press, 1975.

Hill, E. *The Trinidad Carnival: Mandate for a National Theatre*. Austin: University of Texas, 1972.

Salazar, Max. "Latin Music: The Perseverence of a Culture." In *The Puerto Rican Struggle: Essays on Survival in the U.S.*, edited by Clara E. Rodriguez and Virginia Sanchez Korrol, pp. 74-81. New York: Puerto Rican Migration Research Consortium, 1980.

FRANK VALENTICH:
Croatian *Tamburitza* Maker

Doris J. Dyen

For Croatian and Serbian communities in Pennsylvania and throughout America, *tamburitza* music is not just a performing tradition, but a profound symbol of ethnic identity. The music, the instruments, and the dances and songs have had a central role in the traditional cultural life of these communities since the first Yugoslav immigrants began to arrive in the 1880s (see Color Plate #7).

Frank Valentich and his three brothers occupy a special place in the contemporary tamburitza tradition in Pennsylvania. Not only are they musicians with an extensive history of local performing and recording, but they are makers and repairers of the instruments as well—a skill that is becoming increasingly rare. Frank Valentich believes that the two activities go hand in hand and reinforce each other.

> If a cabinet-maker had enough interest to want to build an instrument, there's no reason why he couldn't do it... But to learn what to put *into* it—that's another question! That's what you have to be taught.
>
> Another reason my brothers and I build the best tamburitza instruments is because we're pretty darn good musicians as far as tambura goes. I really think that's an important part of it. We try to fit this thing to some playability. We don't just slap wood together and (say), "Here's an instrument." You can slap it together, but it's not going to have the sound. If you're a musician, you *listen* to other instruments; you say, "Boy, this is a good one! Let me look at this. How did they do this? Yeah, I think that's the way to go." Then you try it out and little by little you develop your own trends of what you want to get out of an instrument. But it comes with time and being interested in it.[1]

With its mines and mills, southwestern Pennsylvania was one of the earliest and strongest centers for Croatian and Serbian immigration. Ethnic churches—Croatian Catholic and Serbian Orthodox—and ethnic clubs were established. Both the Croatian Fraternal Union and the Serb National Federation still maintain their national headquarters in Pittsburgh, and there are local lodges of both organizations throughout the region.

Frank Valentich's father, Marko, came from Selo Selnica, Croatia to the Turtle Creek Valley near Pittsburgh in 1913 to work as a laborer in the Westinghouse Airbrake plant. Typical of many immigrants, he came alone, leaving behind his wife and their infant son John whom he did not see again until 1925 when he had finally saved enough money to pay for their passage and to buy a house. The three younger sons, Joseph, Charles and Frank, were all born in the U.S.

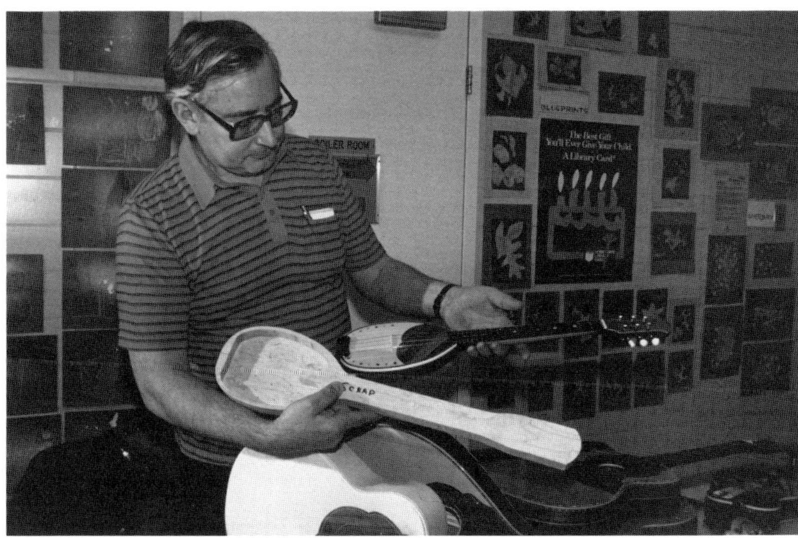

The oldest brother, John, learned metalworking and woodworking and went to work at Westinghouse Electric. During long periods of unemployment in the 1930s, John became an accomplished tamburitza performer, composer and teacher with his father's encouragement and began to experiment with making tamburitza instruments. He taught his brothers Joseph and Charles to play the music, and in the late 1930s they formed an ensemble, the Valentich Brothers Tamburitza Orchestra, which played for local weddings, banquets and club dances, and made some recordings. He also encouraged his younger brothers to learn how to make and repair the instruments. By the late 1940s, when Frank was about 12 years old, both playing and making the instruments were well-established family activities.

When I was a kid, I was making little instruments.... A little miniature thing, about a foot long—I was making a bunch of them.

My brothers (Joe and Charlie) were sort of off on their own, in terms of playing, at the time—they were in their twenties. Joe went into the Duquesne Tamburitzans.... My brother John started a (tamburitza) combo down at Turtle Creek grade school. We had kids of different nationalities there—mostly Cro's and Serbs and that. It was maybe seven or eight of us kids. That was a neat thing. We practiced every Monday night. And I ended up on bass, because we needed a bass player in the family. I was too short to play, so my brother John built me this little stool, six or eight inches high—little me out there with the biggest instrument!

Together the four brothers continued the family craft tradition, with Charles taking the lead and Joseph becoming adept at making strings for the instruments. Frank honed his skills under their direction throughout his teens and twenties, becoming a master craftsman in his own right by the early 1970s.

During the more than fifty years that the Valentich brothers have been making instruments, their craft has evolved in various ways. Although John still builds instruments mainly by hand, Joseph, Charles, and Frank, all machinists, introduced power tools to streamline parts of the process. World War II and continued international political unrest also had an impact on their instrument making. John had made his early instruments of rosewood, but when rosewood became expensive and hard to find the brothers switched to maple which, they discovered, gave a brighter sound. Before the War, John purchased tuning machines from Czechoslovakia, but when trade from Eastern Europe was curtailed, the brothers began making their own tuning machines as well as other tools.

Some changes were introduced through trial and error. Frank notes that for many years, John made instruments year-round and often experienced problems with the untreated wood expanding and contracting.

It's funny my brother John didn't know about this. He's a good mechanic, puts things together very precisely. But his instruments used to crack. So I guess through my brother Charlie's pioneering, he thought, "Hey, you can't make instruments in the summertime!" Where we work, in our home—in the basement—in the summertime, it's humid as heck in the basement. In the wintertime, the furnace kicks on and dries everything out nice, and you've got a place to work.

The brothers have made and repaired all five of the tamburitza instruments, from the smallest to the largest—the *bisernica* or *prim*, and the *brač*, which take the lead melody; the *bugarija*, which plays chords; and the tamburitza cello and bass. Although John made several basses early in his career, the brothers now concentrate on the first four instruments, because the commercially available bass viol has become widely used in tamburitza ensembles. They use maple for the outer body of the instruments, spruce for the bracing and soundboard, and softer woods such as poplar for some of the inner structure.

Many of their instruments contain inlay work. Frank remembers when mother-of-pearl was inexpensive and plentiful, which made it the decorative material of choice, even though it was brittle and hard to shape. One of their favorite designs is a butterfly, which they craft from several colors of mother-of-pearl. Although there is little decorative hand-carving, each of the brothers adapts the standard machined head, where the tuning pegs are fastened, with an extra curlicue or stroke as his special trademark.

The brothers have remained active performers as well. In the early 1960s, Charles, Joseph and Frank formed a second family ensemble, the Tamburitza Serenaders, similar to the Valentich Brothers Orchestra which had disbanded as a result of World War II. Like the earlier group, the Serenaders played for weddings, banquets, Christmas parties and ethnic events.

Right:
The Sloga Tamburitza orchestra plays at a Croatian picnic in the Pittsburgh area. Cokeburg, 1985.

"There were (Croatian) clubs that had music every Saturday and they'd rotate the orchestras—you know, you'd get a chance to play there. And then they'd have the Croatian Day at Kennywood Park—that's been going on for fifty years, probably. And in Duquesne, there's always big doings up at the Croatian Club and the Serbian Club also, on Croatian Day; and then Rankin is a big center for Croatian Day. As I remember the statistics, Croatian Day once brought the biggest number of people into Kennywood Park of any nationality."

The mid-1960s brought a decline in the popularity of tamburitza music, which Frank attributes to a downturn in the economy. It may also be related to a loosening of the old ethnic neighborhood ties, as people moved away to the suburbs. The Serenaders disbanded and Frank joined a "polka-American type" band in 1964, with which he played for 20 years.

The brothers have continued to play tamburitza music together informally, and still meet regularly at each other's homes. Frank characterizes the music they play as "folk stuff," the *bečar* tradition of waltzes, polkas, *kolos* and other dance songs which are partly notated and partly improvised, as distinct from the fully written-out concert-style arrangements played by larger tamburitza orchestras.

In the 1980s, some bečar combos of the old style are still active around the Pittsburgh area, as are several Junior Tamburitza organizations and the Duquesne University Tamburitzans, a famous ensemble which celebrated its fiftieth anniversary in 1988. Although ethnic clubs have lost some of their influence, Croatian Fraternal Union lodges in Pittsburgh and nearby towns such as Ambridge, Cokeburg, McKeesport, and Monessen regularly sponsor events such as lamb roasts, picnics and dances that feature tamburitza music performance. Croatian Catholic churches such as Sacred Heart in McKeesport and St. Nicholas in Millvale have incorporated tamburitza music into their services for special observances.

The efforts of the clubs, churches, and educational programs have nurtured a revival of community interest in tamburitza music and an appreciation for tamburitza musicians. There is thus a small but steady demand for high-quality instrument-making. The Valentich brothers neither advertise nor sell their instruments in commercial music stores; most of their customers are other tamburitza musicians who hear of their work by word-of-mouth.

Frank Valentich is concerned that after his generation there will be no more tamburitza makers in America to contribute to the continuation of Croatian cultural traditions. He would like to find younger people who care about learning to craft the sound as well as perform the music.

Some guys want to play real well, but you can't get them interested in *making* the instruments. It takes a pretty dedicated person to want to do this. A lot of guys, newcomers, say, "I'm going to start building tamburitza instruments." Then when they see how much effort and patience it takes, they quit! I've got two boys—they don't want to participate, cause there's a lot to learn about it, and you have to sit there and do it. It doesn't happen by itself. It's got to come out of the old hands. There's no manual that I know of; what we learned we just passed on to each other.

Notes

1. All quotes are taken from an interview by the author with Frank Valentich, Pittsburgh, March 8, 1988.

Suggested Reading

Bezic, Jerko. "Yugoslavia, II, 3: Folk Music, Croatia." In *The New Grove Dictionary of Music and Musicians*, edited by Stanley Sadie, pp. 596-98 on instruments and dance. London: Macmillan Publishers Ltd., 1980.

Forry, Mark. "European-American Music, III, 12: Yugoslav." In *The New Grove Dictionary of American Music*, edited by H. Wiley Hitchcock and Stanley Sadie, p. 85 on Croatian-Serbian. London/New York: Macmillan Press Ltd./Grove's Dictionaries of Music, 1986.

Gazi, Stjepan. *Croatian Immigration to Allegheny County: 1882-1914*. Pittsburgh: Croatian Fraternal Union, 1956.

Kolar, Walter. *A History of the Tambura, Vol. II: The Tambura in America*. Pittsburgh: Duquesne University Tamburitzans Institute of Folk Art, 1975.

Prpic, George. "The Croatian Immigrants in Pittsburgh." In *The Ethnic Experience in Pennsylvania*, edited by John Bodnar, pp. 263-86. Lewisburg, Pa.: Bucknell University Press, 1973.

THE ALLISON PARK QUILTMAKERS

Doris J. Dyen

"Each person has brought to this group their own bits of personality that they would incorporate into the quilt... They bring to the quilt part of themselves, and they just make the quilt their own." (Fonda Smith)

For the Allison Park Quiltmakers of Hampton Township near Pittsburgh, craftswork has been the catalyst for creating a community of women folk artists, bridging traditional and contemporary attitudes and methods. Members value the club for the sense of mutual encouragement it gives them as well as for the aesthetic satisfaction of producing beautiful pieces of needlework.

As have many quilt clubs in Pennsylvania and throughout the United States, the Allison Park Quiltmakers started fairly recently, following a widespread revival of interest in quilting in the 1970s. Like many clubs, this one also draws from the knowledge of traditional quilting passed down from generation to generation within individual members' families and communities. Fonda Smith, president of the Quiltmakers, remembers how their group began:

> It was in 1982. I had been doing this sort of thing by myself, making quilts and donating them to St. Ursula's Christian Mothers group as fundraisers. And various people would ask me if I would make quilts for them—and I really didn't have the time. Finally I decided this might be a good time to get group involvement. So I said to anyone that was interested, "I will teach you all I know." My knowledge, I knew, was limited, but I did know the basics of quilting, from my mother and my mother-in-law, and because I had participated in a group in the Hampton Presbyterian Church where there were a lot of older ladies. So it was the knowledge that I myself had and my own imagination—I started the group!"

When the Allison Park Quiltmakers started in 1982, there were twenty members. The plant closings of that period forced many families to relocate, and several early members moved away. The club now stays at about a dozen members; it is limited in size because it meets at the home of Fonda Smith. Members range in age from mid-thirties to mid-seventies, with the majority in their forties and fifties. Most are married with teen-aged or adult children.

Most of the original Quiltmakers belonged to St. Ursula's Church in Hampton Township, one of several Catholic congregations in this part of Allegheny County, and over half of the current group are members of this church. Ethnicity does not seem to be a conscious issue among the group; the women are largely of Western European backgrounds—German, Italian, Irish/English, and some French—a typical configuration for rural and exurban communities here. Their families have lived in the southwestern Pennsylvania-West Virginia region for several generations.

Members of the club are middle-class economically and take a traditional approach to family life. Husbands tend to be in business, engineering, or skilled trades, working for local corporations, mills, or public utilities. The women have worked as nurses, secretaries, and teachers, but in many cases, also have spent long periods as full-time homemakers over the years. Group members who are employed at present tend to be part-time workers, which allows them to come to quilting-day meetings and to do vol-

unteer work in the community for Divine Providence Hospital, Meals on Wheels, church missionary activities, literacy programs, and other charitable organizations.

Most of the women had prior experience with needlework before joining the Quiltmakers, but usually it was with undecorated, functional sewing, such as making and mending clothes or curtains. In some cases, quilting was a tradition in the family in earlier times: both Fonda Smith and Carol Gianetti completed quilts begun by older women relatives with skills refined through the Quiltmakers. The club now includes two women who give workshops in quilting and other sewing crafts. For the Allison Park group, though, quilting within the framework of a quilt club is a social and communal cultural expression as well as an individual one. In fact, the intersection of those two dimensions is what intensifies the craft experience for the members.

Several social contexts in which the Quiltmakers participate as a group encourage sharing and interaction and reinforce their sense of

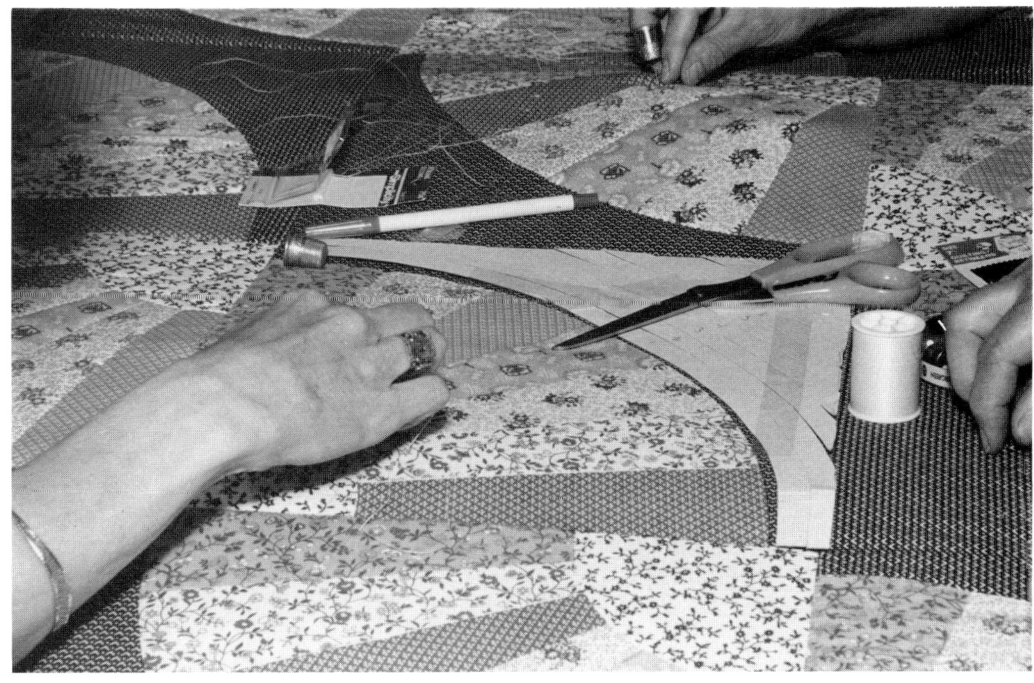

community. The most frequent and regular occasion is the weekly Quilting Day. Members gather every Tuesday from September to June at Fonda Smith's home, from 10:00 a.m. until 2:00 p.m. They usually have coffee together before sitting down to work, and sometimes a member brings doughnuts or sweetrolls for the group. The sewing itself is punctuated by a steady flow of conversation.

At noon, most take their lunch break, which is treated as a separate event within the quilting day. Often the members bring a bag lunch—several members have built up traditions of sharing parts of lunches from home with each other—and Smith usually has cheese and crackers or cut vegetables available for anyone who might not have brought her own lunch that day. Sometimes one member or another will provide lunch for the whole group as a treat, or they will have a potluck lunch, each bringing a covered dish. The lunch break begins with a grace. During the meal there is lively conversation, good-natured bantering, and sympathetic sharing of experiences. Several members have commented on how little outright gossip is exchanged; members value highly their group's ability to maintain a friendly and supportive atmosphere.

The quilt frame, with the current group quilt in progress, is set up in the living room, and members take turns quilting. As many as eight can sit at the frame, but usually just five or six work there at any one time. Other members, seated on the living room couch and chairs or on the floor, work at their own projects, such as lap-quilting a bedcover for a relative or making pillows. The dining room table is used for laying out and marking quilts. Work proceeds informally, and members take time to consult with each other on techniques, colors, and patterns. In addition to the designated group quilt on the frame, individual quilting endeavors can become de facto group projects as members pool their efforts on each other's behalf (see Color Plate #8).

The Quiltmakers sew one group quilt each year. As a group, they select the pattern, then have a shopping day to buy fabric, thread, and template materials. Their first quilt-tops emphasized appliqué and embroidery because these techniques were less complicated than piecing. Smith explains that at first members were encouraged to do the best they could with the skills they had, but recent efforts have included more piecing and more demanding quilting techniques as members' skills have grown.

Each group quilt focuses on solving different technical problems: one was a Victorian white-work (white-on-white quilting), another was completely pieced in the traditional churn-dash pattern, and a third was a sampler with a combination of pieced, appliquéd, and embroidered blocks. The 1988 quilt was made on a pre-printed fabric because of time constraints; for 1989, the group is considering a

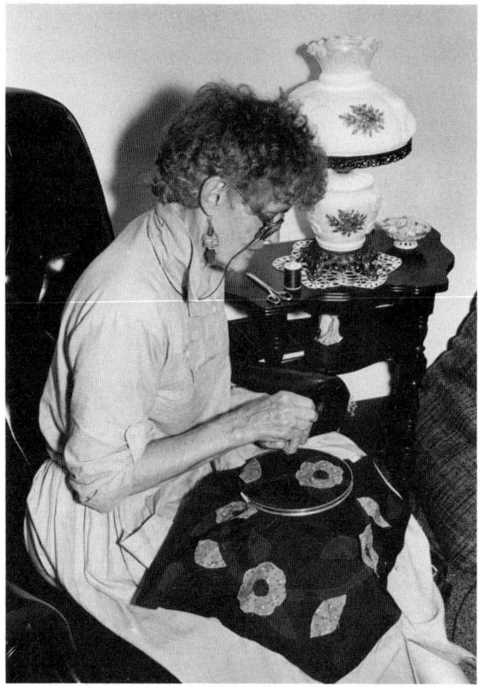

Right:
Eileen Cinicola works on a quilt square featuring appliqué, the technique of hand stitching pieces of fabric on top of each other to create the design. Allison Park, 1987.

"scrap-bag" quilt, for which members will piece the top from fabric scraps and remnants they have been saving in their own workbags.

The women encourage each other to use patterns and techniques passed on to them by other quilters but also to be innovative and resourceful in their sewing. Thus their quilting is an art that continues to evolve out of their collective experience. Although they purchase some of their materials and tools, they also enjoy making up patterns and designing their own piecing and quilting templates. They made some of their early templates from household objects, using strips of wood or cardboard and tracing around the rim of an overturned cup to give the desired shape. They now make many of their templates from a flexible plastic material called "shrinky-dink." Mary Margaret Sullivan, who has a weak left hand, has added a further innovation: gluing sandpaper to the backs of shrinky-dink templates to prevent them from slipping on the fabric during marking. Group members do freehand drawing to develop appliqué pieces, trace pictures from children's coloring books, and experiment with painting on fabric, combining these unconventional techniques with those of traditional quilting.

Various members have developed different skills and interests within the group. Mary Margaret Sullivan and Robbie Seibert are skilled both in traditional piecing and quilting techniques—small stitches and following and designing complicated pieced patterns—and in such alternative techniques as shadow-quilting and echo-quilting. They also are called on to solve the tricky problems of finishing corners or hiding errors. Smith enjoys working with rich and contrasting textured fabrics—silks, velvets, laces. She also introduced the group to the idea of painting pictures on fabric, with which she experimented in her Family History quilt. Mary Lou Wolff

Left:
"Bluebird" appliqué by Mary Margaret Sullivan (checklist #64)

Below:
Templates by Allison Park Quiltmakers. Right: Quilting template for "Interlocking Circles" pattern (checklist #75). Center: Quilting templates for "Squiggle" pattern (checklist #74) and "Interlocking Diamonds" pattern (checklist #76). Left: Piecing template for "Card Tricks" pattern (checklist #73).

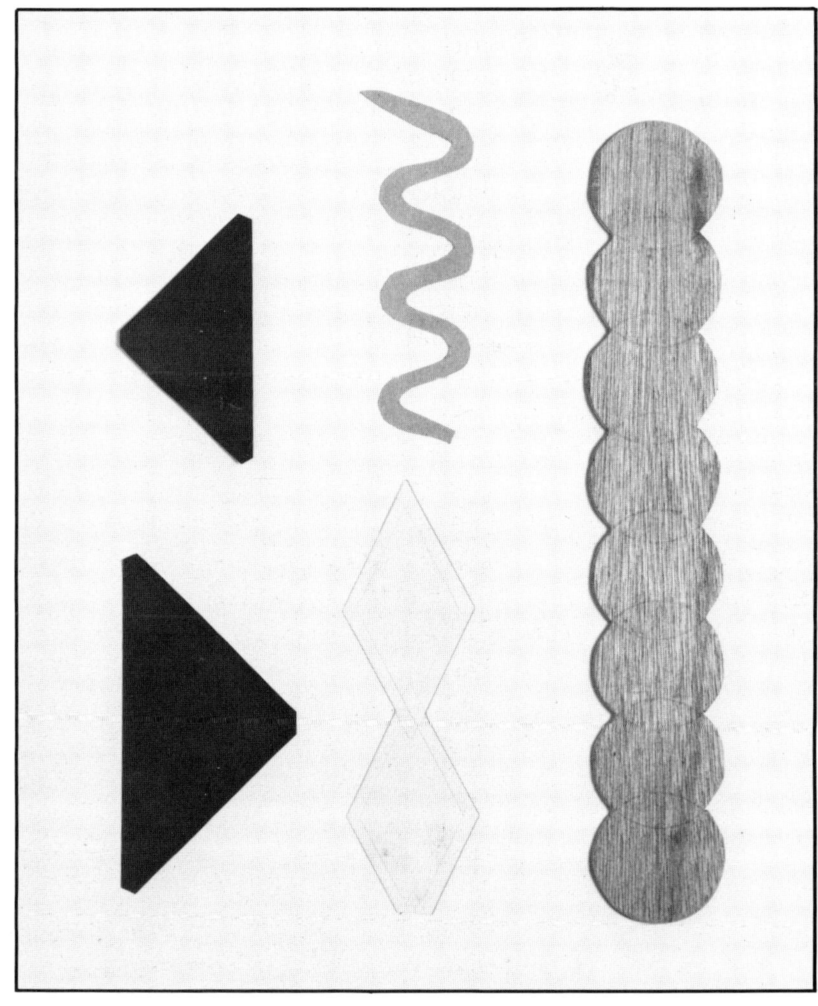

is known within the group for her fine, small stitches.

The quilters enjoy telling anecdotes and jokes and sharing stories as part of their social activities. Recurrent themes include homemaking (house repairs and decorating, relatives' illnesses, and cooking), life-cycle events, or church and community happenings. In the sewing sessions brief anecdotes are interspersed with comments on crafting technique at critical points. During lunch breaks or on social outings there is time to tell longer stories. One of the group's favorites stories—and one which shows their sense of mutual support—is "Helen's First Quilt." Although several members have their own versions of it, that below is Mary Margaret Sullivan's, recorded June 9, 1987.

I'd like to tell you a little story about Helen's first quilt. We made a lovely Victorian quilt two years ago for our church to raffle and the moneys are used for the missions. So Helen said, "I would love to make a quilt like that." She ·was then 75 years old. So we said, why not?—for her Chuckie, her son. Fonda and her husband are very good at enlarging things (for templates), and they took the initials and made great big initials and put them in an oval, and put all these lovely things around the sides and everything for designs. And it was a white-on-white quilt.

But Helen kept worrying that she would die before she got the quilt made! She borrowed one of Fonda's oval frames (for lap-quilting) and made Fonda put her (i.e. Fonda's) name on the frame, "so in case I die, it will come back to you." And we all said, "If you die, Helen, we'll finish the quilt (for you)."

So she sat down to quilt it, and she began to quilt in November—this is a queen-size quilt. And she'd come to club and say, "I don't do anything—I don't make the bed and I don't wash the dishes: I get up in the morning and sit down and start to quilt!" She started just in November, shortly before Thanksgiving.

About two-and-a-half months later, she came with a cake one day, and on the cake it said "I DID IT." The quilt was ready to be bound— she had it all quilted! Of course I thought it, but for once I kept my big mouth shut and didn't say it— but Margaret Bardonner came in and saw it and said, "And you didn't die, Helen!" She didn't die, and now she's working on her second quilt!

The quilters' stories reveal shared attitudes and values which they associate with their craft—values that resemble those ascribed to religious belief and practice: quilting can have healing effects; quilting promotes a sense of caring and commitment to the welfare of others; and quilting reinforces family ties. At the same time, these stories also show the underlying tension that the quilters often feel between their desire to devote time to their craft and their obligation to attend to the daily needs of their homes and families. In an attempt to reconcile this dilemma the Quiltmakers have adopted as their motto "Families First, Quilting Second, Housework Whenever" (an adaptation of the more familiar slogan "Quilting Forever, Housework Whenever"). They also wrote a poem, entitled "Quilter's Syndrome," dealing with this problem, which they printed on the flyleaf of the program for their second show in 1987:

We get up each morning
With a firm new pledge,
We will not quilt today,
But do housework instead.

While dusting the furniture,
Patterns dance through our head
(Well maybe one quick break
before the thought has fled).

We grab the cloth and scissors,
Patterns are scattered all about.
Heavens!! It can't be suppertime
—Guess we'll all eat out.

Families have a special place
In a quilter's heart.
They eat our stews and leftovers
To let us pursue our art.

Our quilts may not be perfect,
But our fingers itch to sew,
Just one more strip of whatever,
To finish out the row.

When a quilter goes to Heaven,
She still has quilter's hopes,
She keeps a needle in her fingers
To quilt St. Peter's robe.

In many ways the Quiltmakers relate to each other as a family and see the group as an extension of their own families. In fact, when the group first started, it actually included several members of the same family. Members of the Quiltmakers look out for and encourage each other, much as they would do with their own kin. At times certain members take on family-like roles toward the rest of the group: Fonda Smith is often "mother" to the group, passing on ideas from "grandmother" (i.e., her own mother, from whom she learned) to the "children" and nurturing the children's skills so that they can become independent craftsworkers on their own. Occasionally, Mary Margaret Sullivan takes on the parental teaching role, instructing the members in a new method or critiquing their efforts. Helen Kolling, 78 years old in 1988, sometimes comments that she is the "grandmother" of the group, bringing a smile from other members who are grandmothers themselves. Yet, at other times Helen takes the role of "child," both because she only recently became a quilter and has had to look to other club members for guidance in learning the craft and because participation in the Quiltmakers has helped her out of a depression so that she actually feels "younger" again.

The idea that quilting strengthens and deepens family cohesion and continuity is expressed not only in the process of quilting, but also in many of the products of the Quiltmakers' efforts. Most of the projects that each individual Quiltmaker sews are functional household items made as gifts for family members, often personalized for the recipient through the incorporation of appliquéd or quilted monograms, favorite motifs, and representational or pictorial forms. For example, the Hunter's Scene quilt was made by Margaret Bardonner as a gift for her husband. Though it is double-bed sized, it is actually a wall-hanging depicting his hunting camp, with a painted scene at the center framed by a quilted white border area.

Often quilts become a means for recording the family's history, functioning somewhat like a photograph album. Margaret Bardonner's first quilt was pieced in a pattern called Autumn Leaves. It incorporates bits of fabric from special clothing of various members of her family "as a means of recalling happy times with them." Fonda Smith, too, has made quilts that incorporate pieces of fabric important in her family's life, such as Lavender and Old Lace, which contains lace from an antique tablecloth that had been in her mother's family. In memory of her mother, Fonda Smith made a Family History quilt comprised of a series of small blocks with quilted borders, each block containing a painted scene. Across the width of the quilt, at the top, she embroidered a caption dedicating the quilt to her mother, Beulah Stonestreet. Her comments about the quilt again intertwine the idea of family continuity with that of quilting as a form of healing:

Below:
"Victorian Roses" quilt by
Mary Lou Wolff, 1986

This was after my mother died, and I just felt the need to preserve some of the things she had told me about the family... And I gave it to the son that had expressed the greatest interest in this sort of thing. My daughter was interested, but the son—this was the most important to him at this time.

This is what I did. I started with the history, the covered wagon, when the family settled in various parts of West Virginia. And I incorporated all this into the quilt, and the crafts that were familiar to them. Hopefully, I got part of their lifestyle down, so it will be a permanent part of the family history... This was something that to me was therapy—this was therapeutic to me, that I could do this and catch some of the memories of some of the things my mother had many times talked with me about...

In some respects, the quilting group creates for its members a strong communal experience, similar to aspects of family interaction and religious community participation. In other respects, the group reinforces the women's associations with their individual families and community networks. These elements can be seen in the other activities and events that the Quiltmakers organize, such as planned social outings. On Fabric Shopping Day, several times a year, the group will make a trip to a fabric store to select materials for new projects. These trips occur on Tuesdays and take the place of that week's Quilting Day. Members go in a car-pool and have a special "lunch out" together.

The annual Quilt Picnic—"that's the time we include the men"—is held in the summer off-season. Each member contributes a covered dish to the meal, and the occasion is a chance for the families of the quilters to get to know each other better.

The Christian Mothers Card Party at St. Ursula's Church is the focus of attention for the annual group-quilting project. During this event, the group quilt is raffled as a benefit for charitable missionary efforts. Many of the members belong to the Christian Mothers group and were friends or acquaintances from that association. In a sense, the quilting club grew out of the Christian Mothers and still acquires new members from that group as well from other religious affiliations and other connections.

The Quilt Shows are times of intense activity for the Allison Park Quiltmakers because they are the public expression of the group's quilting efforts. The club has held shows in 1984 and in 1987 and is planning one for 1989 at the Shaler-North Hills Public Library. The first two shows were benefits for the Depreciation Lands Museum, which focuses on the heritage of the North Hills area including Allison Park and Hampton Township.

The Quilt Shows have heightened the feeling of group identity among the Quiltmakers themselves and have broadened the concept of extended family to include not only relatives of the club members, both male and female, but also other quilters in the community.

The main focus of the Quilt Show is the display of quilts, although other types of needlework may be shown. The quilts include those recently completed by individual members of the Quiltmakers, the most recent group quilt lent for the show by the winner of that year's Christian Mothers raffle, group quilts from earlier years if available, quilts made by relatives, friends, and acquaintances of the Quiltmakers, and antique quilts passed down in the families of the Quiltmakers and the other quilters in the show. Smaller wall-hangings, pillows, and other objects that include quilting, patchwork piecing, or appliqué are also displayed.

A sales area called the "Country Store" offers quilted objects and other forms of needlework. At the 1987 show there was a raffle of a four-poster wooden doll-bed made by Smith's husband Donald, with a quilted bedspread and matching canopy on it sewn by Fonda Smith. In addition, Donald Smith designed and built the frames on which to display the quilts, modeling them on frames he had seen at other quilt shows.

During the shows the Quiltmakers identify themselves publicly as a group in several ways. They have sewn a banner featuring their name and logo (a stylized, grandmotherly-looking woman sitting in a rocking-chair, lap-quilting), which hangs at the entrance to the display area. Each of their group quilts has on the back a label stitched by Helen Kolling with the club name, the date of completion, and a spool of thread. On the show-day the members of the group all wear floor-length cotton dresses and bonnets to give them an old-fashioned look.

Commonly used by groups involved in living-history presentations, local heritage festivals, and similar occasions, this kind of costume has special meaning for the Quiltmakers as a physical statement of their belief that quilting promotes family continuity and, by extension, a community's sense of continuity with its collective past. On the other hand, the group's conscious adoption of an archaic public costume contrasts interestingly with their equally conscious orientation towards the innovative and contemporary in their weekly craftswork activities and their interaction with each other.

Both of the shows have included a small computer-printed checklist with the group's name and logo on the front and a brief description of each numbered item in the show, giving the maker's name, the date the quilt was completed, for whom it was made, and often the meaning of the quilt for the quilter who made it. The 1987 checklist included as well a statement by the Quiltmakers that crystallizes the special meaning quilting holds for them:

> Our present projects will someday be heirlooms. What hopes, dreams and frustrations are worked out in a quilt created for beauty, warmth, and possibly for therapy? The secret is stitched in the quilt forever.

Suggested Reading

Holstein, Jonathan. *The Pieced Quilt: An American Design Tradition.* New York: New York Graphic Society, 1973.

Ferrero, Pat. *Hearts and Hands: The Influence of Women and Quilts on American Society.* San Francisco: The Quilt Digest Press, 1987.

Lasansky, Jeannette. *In the Heart of Pennsylvania: 19th and 20th Century Quiltmaking Traditions.* Lewisburg, Pa.: Oral Traditions Project of the Union County Historical Society, 1985.

__________. *Pieced by Mother: Over 100 Years of Quiltmaking Traditions.* Lewisburg, Pa.: Oral Traditions Project of the Union County Historical Society, 1987.

Lasansky, Jeannette, ed. *In the Heart of Pennsylvania: Symposium Papers.* Lewisburg, Pa.: Oral Traditions Project of the Union County Historical Society, 1986.

__________. *Pieced by Mother: Symposium Papers.* Lewisburg, Pa.: Oral Traditions Project of the Union County Historical Society, 1988.

Lithgow, Marilyn. *Quiltmaking and Quiltmakers.* New York: Funk & Wagnalls, 1974.

Safford, Carleton L. and Robert Bishop. *American Quilts and Coverlets.* New York: E.P. Dutton & Co., Inc., 1980.

BOB ROCK:
Blacksmith

Malachi S.
O'Connor

Bob Rock has been a blacksmith and tool maker in Bedford County, Pennsylvania, for almost sixty years. Born in 1906 and raised on a farm, Rock expected to buy his own farm after he married Sarah Grove in 1928. Finding the cost of available farms to be more than they were willing to pay, Rock heard about a blacksmith who wanted to sell his house and shop. The price was right, and he purchased the shop, house, and two acres in 1929. Rock bought a hand crank forge from Sears and Roebuck, borrowed an anvil, and began tinkering in the shop, making screw drivers and bending iron. While he was making a stove poker for himself, one of his neighbors admired it and asked Rock to make one for him too. This exchange marked the beginning of Rock's role in the community as someone on whom people rely to make and repair all sorts of tools (see Color Plate #3).

When Rock began his work as a blacksmith, horses were still a major mode of power for farm equipment and travel. He shod horses for thirty years in his shop and on farms throughout the area. When the gas tractor entered the Snake Spring Valley region in the 1930s, Rock adapted to the change and began to make and repair farm equipment to be used with tractors. His most successful innovation was the "Rock wagon," an all-purpose farm wagon which used I-beam axles and car wheels for the running gear. If a customer desired, he would put a wooden bed on the chassis, using lumber that he cut and ran through his own sawmill. Over the years Rock made and numbered 404 Rock wagons, and his wife painted almost all of them.

A musician and banjo maker as well as a blacksmith, Bob Rock made his first banjo when he was about ten years old. He ripped a loose paling from a farm fence and attached to it the lid of a can. He whittled wooden pegs for this homemade instrument and used dynamite wire for strings. There were no frets on the banjo, but as he learned a song, Rock would mark the location of each note on the banjo neck. Rock, his neighbor Walt Diehl, and a couple of other friends began playing for local barn dances when they were about twelve years old. Rock, who has been playing ever since, still performs weekly with the "Happy Senior Citizens' Band" at senior citizens' homes in Bedford and Fulton Counties.

Below:
Bob and Sarah Rock sit on their front porch while Bob plays a "Big Chief" banjo, one of three styles of five-string banjos he makes and sells as a hobby. Everett, 1988.

Although Rock calls blacksmith-ing his "work" and banjo making his "hobby," he has made and sold over four hundred banjos and currently devotes equal amounts of time to each pursuit. Blacksmithing and banjo making may seem to be unre-lated processes, but they comple-ment and overlap each other in Rock's working world. Both are or-ganized around the innovative de-sign of tools and work techniques that make creative use of available materials; and both are part of larger personal and community contexts of thrift and cohesion.

Early in Rock's career as a blacksmith, for example, a forest ranger, whose picks, shovels, and axes Rock regularly sharpened, was planting Chinese Chestnut trees on a nearby mountainside and offered him some saplings. Fifty years later Rock cut some of the trees, and used the lumber for banjo drums and resonators. These ban-jos, of his own design, are also made from local sassafras, walnut, and cherry trees. Wood for the shop he built in 1938 similarly came from local trees left by lumbermen at the side of a nearby creek. Rock still sharpens tools for road crews, tele-phone pole installers, and others, often at no charge. In return he re-ceives scrap metal, which he trans-forms into useful objects. Some pieces of scrap metal become tone rings and flanges for his banjos; oth-ers become carving knives or blacksmithing material. Rock then passes on his savings to his cus-tomers. Banjo parts cost him less to make than if he had purchased them from a supplier so he can charge less for the finished product than most banjo manufacturers and still make a profit. Through his own thrift Rock acquires more custom-ers as word spreads of his high-quality workmanship and reason-able prices. Customers who stop by to see the banjos and play music come to rely on him for banjos, strings, straps, and camaraderie.

Blacksmith work is primarily repair work, which is often more complicated than new construction. In order to repair a piece of equipment, Rock must understand the methods of its design and manufacture and its intended use; he must act as an engineer as well as a mechanic.[1] One local farmer, who brought plow points to Rock to be repaired and welded, did not understand why they had worn so quickly. Drawing on years of his own local farming experience, Rock explained to him that the factory attached the points to the manufactured plows at an incorrect angle for the specific soil conditions in Bedford County.

Often, Rock's knowledge of the ways materials act under different conditions leads to innovations in repair work. His reputation in the community is built and maintained on his creative solutions to technological problems, such as his method of straightening axles that have hit rocks or other obstacles in the field. Many farm equipment repair shops bring axles back into line by heating them with a torch at the bent point and then straightening them while the metal is hot. Because this heating process permanently softens the metal, Rock has designed axle straighteners with which he can true or bend axle while the metal is cold. One of the straighteners is an old railroad rail bender that Rock modified for use in his workbench vise. For larger wagon alignment problems he designed and made a frame out of scrap pieces of I-beam in which a wagon can sit and be straightened with the assistance of a "come-along." As with many of his innovations, Rock originally set out with one idea in mind and gradually developed something else during the process of the tool's manufacture. In this case as he began to make a metal pressing device, Rock realized the tool's potential for pulling axles back into line and changed his plans. His intimate understanding of metal and wood—how they will expand or contract in heat or cold and how they can be weakened or strengthened—contributes to Rock's success as an innovative repair man.

Below:
Banjo by Bob Rock
(checklist #87)

Rock's understanding is perhaps nowhere more clearly evident than in his re-use of available scrap. Not only does he rarely throw anything away, Rock also makes regular trips to the dump where he finds and salvages all sorts of usable materials. He uses pieces of scrap metal in the manufacture of tools as well as repair parts. For instance, Rock made from scrap one tool to bend U-bolts and another to turn flat pieces of iron and steel into circular hoops for such things as barrels and banjos.

Like other innovative and experienced mechanics, Rock has the uncanny ability to see the whole project in his mind's eye and invent tools and methods to streamline the work processes. Clamping frets on the fret board of a banjo neck demands painstaking and meticulous work. Rock had been clamping each fret by hand using "C" clamps when he saw a fret press on a visit to a banjo factory in Athens, Ohio. He then returned to his shop and ingeniously made his own press out of scrap materials. This tool, modeled after the one he had seen, improved on the design and cost him only his time.

Before proceeding to solve the problem at hand, an innovative mechanic surveys his resources of available tools and scrap materials. His understanding is structural. The available resources of past experience do not necessarily bear a direct connection to his current projects or to any particular project. Yet, it is from the rules for action generated from the relations among these resources that decisions are made about how to approach the current situation.[2] When Rock needed a rip saw and decided to make one, he scanned his supply of scrap materials and parts. His strategy included using the legs from a piece of machinery he found at the dump for the base of the saw. He already had a two-horsepower motor, which once had powered the line shaft at a shoe repair shop nearby. He turned the mandrill, on which the saw's blade

spins, on his lathe, and he made a "butcher block" table for the saw from his supply of maple and walnut. For the rip fence, the guide that dictates the width of a cut, he took part of a machine previously used in a barrel stave mill. To make his rip saw, then, Rock merged his understanding of materials with the ability to think in design engineering terms. Generally, that merger provides an environment in which he can foresee possible future transformations and reconnections of scrap material as parts of whole objects.

In Bob Rock's mechanical world tools and materials are continually changing shape. He not only makes new tools to serve his purposes, he modifies existing tools to perform certain tasks more carefully and efficiently. Almost every power tool in Rock's shop has undergone some modification over the years. One drill press has a specially designed flywheel, and his workbench vise has specially welded jaws designed to hold sawblades while sharpening them.

Above:
Bob Rock press-fits frets on a banjo neck. He made the press, designed to work accurately at any angle, completely from scrap materials. Everett, 1988.

jects. At a time when industrialized work has been rationalized and compartmentalized into tiny pieces and planners and designers separated from makers and doers, it is unusual to find a person who carries through an entire work process from design, through manufacture, to use.

Beyond his work life Rock's work with materials influences his mental outlook, and together they shape what can be termed a "mechanical worldview."[4] Douglas Harper, following Levi-Strauss, describes this movement from the material to the mental:

> It is not only that the work solves material problems, but also that one's life choices take on the same characteristics as the decisions made in the course of work. It is in the replication of the means that the material work influences the mental.[5]

Rock often manufactures jigs, guides for repeated cuttings or bendings.[3] Jigs expand the functional repertoire of a tool, allowing it to perform all sorts of tasks it would not appear to be able to do. For example, Rock uses a jig of his own design to cut grooves in the metal restraining hoops that fasten the head of a banjo to the banjo drum. Without the jig, the same metal cutting-saw blade is used in a more conventional way for an unconventional purpose, the cutting of old and rusted two-man saws into pieces for butcher knife blades. Rock's understanding of materials and of what tools can do, the product of years of experience, is flexible and continually growing.

Behind every object Bob Rock makes are tools used to make that object, whether it is a banjo or a farm wagon. More than a craftsman who makes and repairs things that people need, Rock is a designer and manufacturer of customized tools to make and repair those ob-

Rock's work with materials and design problems influences his understanding of how the world works. His years of everyday economic transactions within the community have social as well as monetary significance. Many customers have mentioned that Rock has taught them how to save money by repairing and using a given tool creatively and correctly and, at the same time, has taught them the importance and value of thrift in their everyday lives.

In both his personality and his work, Rock embodies an economy of thrift. In agricultural communities, such as the one described here, work is more than the means by which one makes a monetary living; it is the "currency of community," the center of many sorts of social as well as economic exchange.[6] The reputations and livelihoods of farmers and the local blacksmith were mutually interdependent in the past because farmers rarely could afford to buy a new tool whenever an old one broke down. For the same reason, farmers now take repair work to their local farm equipment dealer. In Bedford County, however, both farmers and equipment dealers are fortunate to still have a local blacksmith. When the John Deere dealer cannot repair or locate parts for one of his own products, he sends the customer to Rock's shop. Rock is known throughout the community as a craftsman who can repair anything from radios and watches to any metal or wooden object.

Rock's relationship with the community is a complicated one. People depend on him to forge solutions to their technological problems, and in return he has achieved status in the community as a special person. Work relations are bound together with social relations and obligations as well. To see the business transaction as one involving only the exchange of labor for money is to miss the larger point.

Below:
Bob Rock welds plow points at the angle best suited for long-term use on the tractors of local farmers working fields in the Snake Spring Valley. Everett, 1988.

The social and economic context in which Bob Rock works is one of community thrift. Rock's shop remains in many ways at the hub of a pattern of technological interaction within the community, with repair problems entering the shop and solutions leaving to be implemented upon return to the farm.

Agricultural life is composed of periods of intense activity punctuated by periods of more loosely structured time and so is the life of the blacksmith whose clients are farmers.[7] Planting, cultivating, and harvesting must be accomplished according to the dictates of climate and weather. While some periods in the agricultural cycle are slower than others, work never ends for the farmer or the blacksmith. As Rock says, "I don't stop; I just keep going, always working."[8] If he is not repairing agricultural equipment, he is building banjos or making knives.

Rock says he is puzzled when people ask him how many hours it takes to make a banjo. He, like the farmer, does not measure his work in quantities of clock time but by the demands of the work at hand. Time is embedded in the task, and the "specific nature of the job determines the duration of the work."[9] It does not matter how much time it takes to sow corn in a field. Corn must be sown when the time is ripe, according to the dictates of climate and weather. Corn planting tools, by extension, must be ready to work at that time. If they do not work correctly, there will be no harvest. Repair men such as Bob Rock must be prepared to put those tools in working order in time for planting to take place.

The pace of agricultural time does not ignore the clock although Rock does not believe in what he calls "fast time." As he puts it, "When the sun comes up an hour earlier, I'll get up an hour earlier."[10] A steady working rhythm, punctuated by intermittent periods of intensity, affords Rock time to talk with custom-

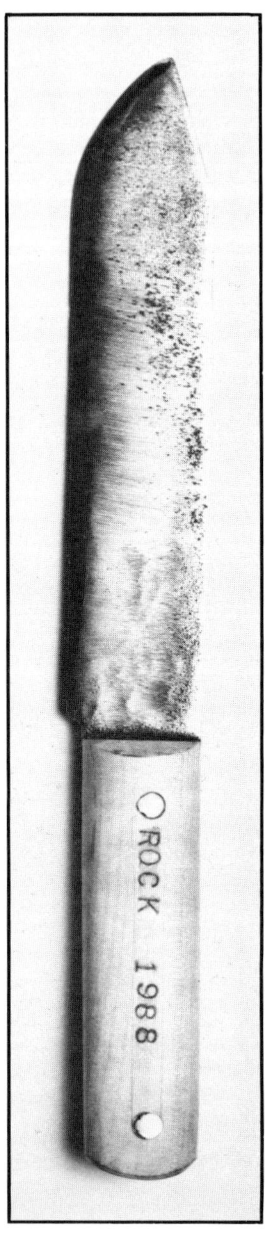

Above:
Knife by Bob Rock
(checklist #78)

ers and time to pass news through the community circuit. Rock's shop, as an extension of his personality and role in the community, provides a context for this type of interaction to take place. When old customers bring repair work into the shop, they make time to exchange stories about the latest happenings in the community. When old friends and neighbors drop by, there is time to talk about life in the old days: of hunting, of early cars, of barn dances when they were youngsters, and of Rock's "getting a good deal," performing an interesting athletic feat, or treating a neighbor fairly.

There are many stories Rock and others tell about his getting a good deal. He is in some respects not unlike the traditional Yankee trader. When Rock went to see Shan Mortimer about buying his house, for example, his car tire went flat outside the blacksmith's shop. Of course Mortimer came out to the road to help him repair it. Rock had heard that the blacksmith wanted to sell and was visiting him for that reason, but he did not talk about Mortimer's house directly. Instead Rock chatted about a farm he had just turned down because it was too expensive. Mortimer mentioned that his own house was for sale, and Rock said he was not too interested. Then, as they completed work on the tire, Rock asked Mortimer what he would take for his house. He said Rock could have it for $925, and Rock answered, he recalls, "I'll just take her, right away before he [Shan Mortimer] changed his mind."[11]

Rock is well known in the community as a runner. Many people tell the story of the time Rock, then in his late seventies, drove his car five miles into the town of Bedford to have it repaired. When the repairman turned around to tell him he could pick it up later that afternoon Rock was gone. He ran all the way home. Rock tells many running stories about himself and about his neighbors' opinion that he is "bull-

headed" for running at the age of 82. He still challenges new customers to a footrace and says he has been beaten only once. He also challenges people to lifting contests. He tells a story about a 247 pound pattern block that he bought for only one dollar, lifted, and carried to his truck without getting his Sunday suit dirty.

Rock's shop is a neighborhood resource as well the location for social interaction. One neighbor, who drives a tractor trailer, parks his truck next to the shop because he does not have enough room in his own driveway. Rock relies on another neighbor for assistance in bending and clamping wooden strips for banjo drums after they have been boiled. In exchange, that neighbor has full access to the shop at any time. Rock has guided this neighbor as he made a banjo for himself. Other neighbors call on Rock whenever they need anything repaired, and Rock knows he can call on them whenever he needs help.

Rock's reputation in the community has been built through his sixty years of work as a blacksmith and banjo maker. He does not retire in part because he loves to work. Moreover, he feels a responsibility to the community. Rock says he would not retire even if he wanted to because "I made my money in the community, and there is no one else around here doing this kind of work."[12] Members of the community echo this sentiment when they wonder aloud what the community will do when Rock stops working. They often express their frustration that no one in the community is learning and continuing Rock's work. These sentiments offer further testimony that, in a local economy of thrift, Bob Rock and his blacksmith shop occupy a prominent position at the heart of a balanced pattern of reciprocal community relations.

Notes

1. Douglas Harper, *Working Knowledge, Skill and Community in a Small Shop* (Chicago: University of Chicago Press, 1987), pp. 4, 19-21, 73.

2. Claude Levi-Strauss, *The Savage Mind* (Chicago: University of Chicago Press, 1966), p. 21.

3. John T. Schlebecker, *Whereby We Thrive, A History of American Farming, 1607-1972* (Ames: The Iowa State University Press, 1978), p. 76.

4. For further discussion of the concept of "mechanical worldview," see Malachi O'Connor, "Playful Work: Avocation and the Commemoration of a Mechanical Worldview" (Ph.D. diss., University of Pennsylvania, 1988).

5. Harper, *Working Knowledge*, p. 75.

6. Ibid., p. 7.

7. E.P. Thompson, "Time, Work-Discipline and Industrial Capitalism," *Past and Present* 38(1967):73.

8. Interview with Bob Rock, June, 1988.

9. Harper, *Working Knowledge*, p. 136.

10. Interview with Bob Rock, June, 1988.

11. Interview with Bob Rock, April, 1986.

12. Interview with Bob Rock, June, 1988.

Suggested Reading

Glassie, Henry. *Passing the Time in Ballymenone*. Philadelphia: University of Pennsylvania Press, 1982.

Mumford, Lewis. *Technics and Civilization*. New York: Harcourt, Brace, Jovanovich, 1963.

Pye, David. *The Nature and Aesthetics of Design*. New York: Van Nostrand, Reinhold, Company, Inc., 1978.

Smith, H.R. Bradley. *Blacksmiths' and Farriers' Tools at Shelburne Museum— A History of Their Development from Forge to Factory*. Shelburne, Vt.: The Shelburne Museum, Inc., 1966.

Sturt, George. *The Wheelwright's Shop*. New York: Cambridge University Press, 1976.

Sudnow, David. *Ways of the Hand: The Organization of Improvised Conduct*. Cambridge: Harvard University Press, 1978.

Toelken, Barre. "Folklore, Worldview, and Communication." In *Folklore: Performance and Communication*, edited by Dan Ben-Amos and Kenneth S. Goldstein, pp. 265-86. The Hague: Mouton, 1975.

HICKORY FURNITURE MAKERS IN SOUTHWESTERN PENNSYLVANIA

Shalom D. Staub[1]

Before the days of craft shops and mail-order craft catalogues, crafts-workers generally gathered and prepared the materials they used locally. Craftswork depended upon the availability of natural resources, and the worker's ability to shape those raw materials into functional, and often aesthetically pleasing, objects. Many craft traditions are highly localized, due to the limited availability of particular resources, for example the sweet grass baskets made along the Carolina coast or the pounded ash pack baskets in the Adirondacks.[2] The flora and fauna of a region, its geography and natural resources are all intimately related to the development and continuity of a craft tradition.

This essay examines one of Pennsylvania's regionally based crafts traditions: hickory furniture making in Bedford and Somerset counties, southwestern Pennsylvania. The terrain here is mountainous, with high ridges and deep valleys typical of the Allegheny highlands, part of the Appalachian chain cutting through Pennsylvania from the southwest to the northeast. The counties are sparsely populated, dispersed mainly in small farms and villages. Residents in this rural area are mostly of German, English, and Irish Protestant descent; Methodist, Lutheran, Brethren, and United Church of Christ congregations dot the rural landscape. Amish and Mennonite communities are also present.[3] Unemployment in the counties has been high in recent years. Young people often leave the area for jobs in nearby Johnstown, Altoona and Pittsburgh. Coal mines, sheep farms, and grist mills once dominated the occupational profile of the region. Now, dairy and sheep farming, forestry, factory work and the tourism and recreation industry provide a livelihood for many residents. Crops are planted and harvested throughout the hilly terrain, while large stands of timber dominate the steeper hillsides.

Hickory and oak abound in this region, and area woodworkers have used these available resources to fashion furniture as far back as 1850, according to current craftsworkers' family histories.[4] The catalogue for Davis & Wentz Hickory Furniture of New Paris states:

> The Davis family has been making hickory rocking chairs since the mid 1800s when John W. Davis made his first Hickory rocking chair and began what was to become a family tradition of making hand-crafted hickory furniture.
>
> The art of making these beautiful chairs has been handed down through four generations and perfected to obtain what we believe to be the highest quality and finest workmanship available in hand-crafted hickory furniture.

John W. Davis reportedly made the "first" hickory rocker when his wife asked him for a comfortable chair for nursing her baby. To this day, a common local custom is to buy newlyweds a hickory rocker. In fact, the height for the rocker's arm is often determined by the distance which is comfortable for a woman to place her elbow while rocking and nursing a baby.

Above:
Hickory rocker by Lee Woida (checklist #89)

Right:
Hickory branches are stored outside the Davis and Wentz furniture shop until ready for molding and assembly. New Paris, 1986.

Of the fifty or more varieties of hickory in the world, five grow in the Bedford-Somerset area. The hickory used for furniture making has great hardness, pliability owing to its small pith, and durability due to a bark which does not peel off with age. Depending on its location, hickory is harvested in the fall when the sap is down after three to five years of growth. At this age, hickory trees are one to two inches thick. Modern hickory furniture is easy to identify, because the wood from young trees quickly tapers from its wider base to a narrow tip. Older hickory furniture, built with virgin hickory, used mature trees of more uniform thickness.

Craftsworkers may acquire hickory either for cash—paying from fourteen to twenty cents per tree, in exchange for a finished chair, or by growing it themselves on their own land. Harvested hickory is then dried for six months to a year before it can be used. Some craftsworkers maintain that hickory must be stored in the dark to discourage damage from larval worms which would cause the wood to lose its pliability and possibly crack during bending. The largest of the hickory furniture shops in this region uses 8,000 hickory trees per year.

Left:
Before shaping the wood in a jig, Lee Woida steams the slats in a boiler to make them soft and pliable. Fairhope, 1986.

Below:
Abraham Latshaw shapes the oak slats used for the chair back with a specially designed jig. New Paris, 1985.

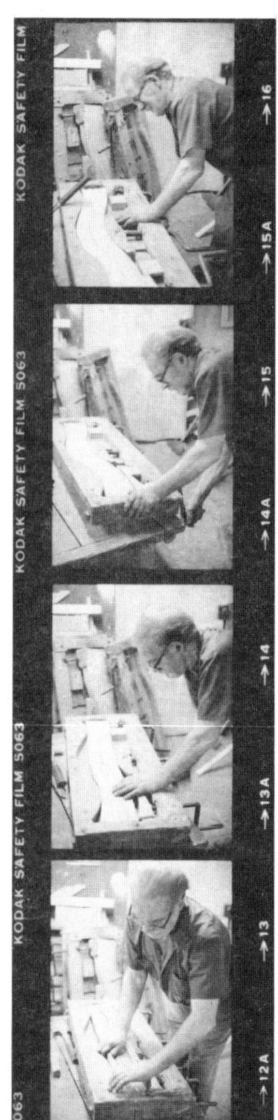

Among the commonly made types of hickory furniture are rocking chairs, straight chairs with and without arms, porch swings, settees, footstools, desks, and dining, coffee and end tables. The most common item by far is the hickory rocker, actually constructed of hickory and oak.[5] The rough bark of the hickory, which insures that no two chairs will look exactly alike, provides the fundamental structure of the chair: the front and back legs, the seat hoop, the posts which create the frame for the back slats, and the arms. The seat slats and seat frame, back slats and the rockers are made from oak. Rocking chairs are made in various sizes, ranging from a rocker built for two, adult sizes from small to extra large, a child's size, and even baby doll rockers.

Techniques of building the rocker vary somewhat among craftsworkers in the region, yet all share some basic methods and tools. For example, a large, rectangular, metal boiler is used to boil or steam the wood to make it pliable for shaping. Hickory is boiled for approximately fifteen minutes, while oak is steamed for about thirty minutes. These two woods are usually not boiled together, since the hickory would cause the oak to turn black. Craftsworkers in this region commonly use homemade wooden jigs to bend the boiled or steamed wood into predetermined shapes for particular parts of the chair, though the jigs themselves vary considerably. All use power rotary and jig saws.

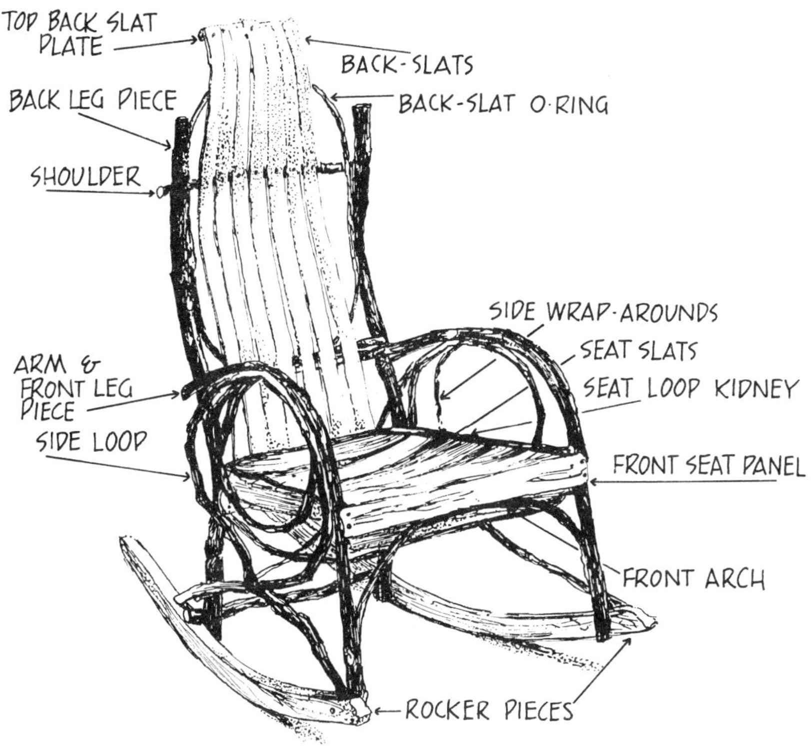

Above:
Ink drawing by Diane Zatz showing hickory chair construction, 1988

Below:
Lee Woida, hickory furniture maker, in his shop. Fairhope, 1986.

Most of the hickory craftsworkers begin constructing their chairs by joining the front and back leg posts to the seat hoop. The front leg posts bend to form the chair arms, attaching to the rear posts below midpoint. The rear leg posts extends upward in a curved shape to establish the contour for the back rest. A form is used to steady the legs, and also functions to standardize the distances between leg posts, front braces, and the seat hoop. Temporary braces are then nailed across all key joints to brace the chair's curvilinear form during assembly. Pre-shaped oak slats are nailed onto a curved seat frame to produce the characteristic dip in the seat. Additional oak slats are then added to form the seat back. Pre-bent loops and half-circles of hickory are added to the arm sections, the lower side sections down to the rockers, and on the back. The last structural element of the assembly is attaching the rockers. Sanding generally occurs at this stage, although some craftsworkers like to pre-sand the oak slats. All pieces of the chair are attached by nails: oak to oak, oak to hickory, and hickory to hickory. When nailing through hickory, holes are pre-drilled to prevent splitting the wood or bending the nails. Care is taken to clinch the protruding nails. Disc sanders are used to smooth the nobby areas where branches had grown on the hickory. After the final sanding, the rocker is varnished with polyurethane.

While this construction technique is commonly practiced, and in fact viewed by the majority of furniture makers as the norm for the region, some craftsworkers have adopted other techniques through experimentation. Viewed as "primitive" by those practicing the technique described above, the alternative construction techniques work quite well. Lee Woida, age 34, has been making hickory rockers for fourteen years. He learned from his grandfather Gus, who was eighty

Left:
After the chair frame is made and the back slats have been shaped in the boiler, Lee Woida nails the slats on to the frame. Fairhope, 1986.

Below:
Bennie Zook, Amish furniture maker, nails the seat slats on to the frame. Meyersdale, 1986.

years old at the time. Gus Woida, of Russian-German descent, wanted to get into the hickory furniture business, but the secrecy among local craftsworkers prevented him from learning any established techniques. Through trial and error, he developed his own approach, which he later taught to his grandson Lee, a former house painter from New Jersey. Lee Woida knows that others think his methods unusual, even incomprehensible, but he takes pride in continuing his grandfather's legacy.

Woida uses jigs as well as the steamer, but instead of trimming the hickory branches with a power jig saw, he uses forceful strokes with a hand-held knife. When he begins the chair assembly, the major difference of technique becomes apparent. Woida builds his chairs from the "bottom up." He begins by laying out the rockers, inserting the front and rear posts, then building the seat support, and finally attaching the oak slats.

From the way other crafts-workers in the region talk, Woida's technique would seem idiosyncratic; but this is not the case. The Amish proprietor of Bennie's Hickory Rocker Chair Shop in Somerset County employs essentially the same construction technique, with yet further variation. While this chair maker uses jigs to bend the oak slats and the hickory support posts, he does not pre-bend the distinctive hickory loops and circles. After the chair is framed with the oak slats attached, Bennie fires up the steamer and heats six pieces of hickory for approximately twenty minutes. He pulls each one out individually, bends it to the appropriate shape, and tacks it directly onto the rocker. The hickory dries into its bent shape attached to the assembled chair.

Whether one works from the sides inwards and downwards or from the bottom up, whether one uses power tools or hand tools, or whether one employs jigs or shapes the hickory by hand, the resulting hickory rockers are structurally identical to each other. All of these different techniques work, in part because they are appropriate to the scale of the individual craftsworker's operation. Davis & Wentz are probably the most prolific traditional hickory furniture makers in the region, utilizing their relatively mechanized procedures with pre-shaped oak and hickory to make roughly seven hundred items per year. Woida and Bennie each produce roughly 350 to 400 chairs per year, considerably less than Davis & Wentz combined but enough to support their families and live as they wish in this rural area.

More than a dozen craftsworkers are making hickory furniture in the Bedford-Somerset area. Competition, both for resources and for customers, is intense. Neighboring craftsworkers, living not more than a mile from each other, may avoid discussing business and certainly will not mention techniques. There is suspicion and secrecy, owing to a concern for protecting one's business interest. Outsiders expressing interest in the production of hickory chairs are viewed with skepticism by some furniture makers who feel that their past generosity may have later hurt their business.

Each chair maker tries to establish his own market. Due to the size of their operation, Davis & Wentz can sell to stores out of the region and fill mail orders. Before Abraham Latshaw died in 1986, he supplied chairs for mail orders from the Orvis catalogue. Woida travels to arts festivals and crafts fairs, demonstrating his chairmaking to attract potential buyers.

For Bennie, chairmaking became an attractive occupation when he married about twelve years ago and his brother inherited the family farm. Bennie had tried tenant farming but did not find that satisfying. His wife's family was running a successful hickory chair shop in New Castle, Pennsylvania, near the Ohio border, so Bennie spent some time with his sister-in-law's family to learn the trade. His decision to become a furniture maker was the result of a family discussion concerning strategies for economic survival. His chairmaking allows him to be close to his family and preserve his commitment to personal and community values.

One market for hickory chairs is local. Bedford and Somerset County restaurants and hotels are commonly furnished with locally produced chairs and tables. Local residents take pride in their regional furniture tradition. Amish families, both local and those in other parts of the country, purchase hickory rocking chairs through a network of Amish shops such as Bennie's.

Another market extends well beyond the immediate folk cultural communities, based on shared region and religion, to respond to the national popular culture demand for the "country" look. The unpeeled hickory bark imparts a symbolic quality of back country living and belies the careful measurements and the use of standardizing jigs in the chair's assembly. In fact, marketing strategies may emphasize this aspect of the chair's appeal. The Latshaw's furniture catalogue is subtitled "Rustic Furniture Since 1948" and features a pen and ink drawing of the interior of a hunting cabin. The hickory rocker is situated in the center of the image, with a golden retriever lying before the chair. A fireplace is off to the right, and to the left, a hickory table with a presumably handcarved duck decoy. An image of a framed fishing trophy photograph hangs on the back wall, along with other, suitably country-like accoutrements.

The survival of hickory chairmaking as a viable craft depends on the craftsworker's ability to meet, and even develop this popular market. With his appearances at crafts fairs, Lee Woida has been able to generate for himself local media attention, and similarly, the Latshaws have benefited from media coverage in *Time* and *Country Living*. In some respects, the chairmakers produce an image as much as they create the tangible object, for the hickory rocker's popular appeal is surely tied both to its comfort and its nostalgic, old-time country aesthetic. Still intimately connected to the Bedford-Somerset region, its natural resources and its people, hickory furniture making is a craft which now transcends its regional boundaries.

Left:
Latshaw Furniture Catalog
(checklist #100)

Notes

1. This essay is based on fieldwork reports prepared by Shalom Staub, Richard Vidutis, Geraldine Johnson, Malachi O'Connor, and Doris Dyen.

2. Dale Rosengarten, *Row Upon Row: Sea Grass Baskets of the South Carolina Low Country* (Columbia, S.C.: McKissick Museum, 1987); Henry Glassie, "William Houck, Maker of Pounded Ash Adirondack Packbaskets," *Keystone Folklore Quarterly* 12 (Spring 1967):23-54. Immigrant groups often find that their customary materials are unavailable in their new environment. Sometimes such groups abandon those crafts which are most dependent on the natural resources of their homeland; for example, bamboo crafts of the Hmong are rarely practiced in the U.S. Often, however, individuals adapt new materials to perpetuate a traditional form, as in the case of plastic straps replacing the bamboo of Hmong baskets noted in Sally Peterson's essay.

3. There are small Polish and Italian American communities in Somerset County, and an Afro-American community in the borough of Bedford.

4. Family histories of craftsworkers Harry Davis and Abraham Latshaw place the "origins" of hickory chairmaking to this time.

5. The hickory rocker is made with either oak or walnut by Davis & Wentz, and in oak exclusively with no hickory by Roger Lamens.

Suggested Reading

Glassie, Henry. *Pattern in the Material Folk Culture of the Eastern United States.* Philadelphia: University of Pennsylvania Press, 1968.

Jones, Michael Owen. *The Hand Made Object and Its Maker.* Berkeley: University of California Press, 1975.

THE ETHICS OF CRAFTSMANSHIP AMONG THE LANCASTER COUNTY AMISH*

Malachi S.
O'Connor

The first substantial Amish settlement in Lancaster County began in the Pequea Valley in the early 1800s. The settlers brought with them from the Alsace and Palatinate regions of Europe by way of Berks County a tradition of family farming that continues to be the backbone of Amish life to this day. The Amish take as their mandate the biblical commands that they be stewards of the land owned by the Lord (I Corinthians, 10:26) and that they remain separate from the world (Romans, 12:2). Because the Amish view the land as a gift that is theirs to use, improve, and pass on to the next generation, farming lies at the center of everyday religious and work life.

For many of us in the modern world our sacred and secular lives are quite separate. This is not so for the Amish, whose work and religious beliefs are inseparably entwined. In Amish life sacred ritual is embedded in the every-day activities of work, dress, and family relations.[1] In such common, everyday activities the sacred power that undergirds creation is revealed, and "participants incarnate or manifest that power."[2] For the Old Order Amish, "planting and harvesting are as sacred in their own ways as singing and praying"[3] (see Color Plate #9).

In their everyday working lives the Amish enact their belief in humility. The purpose of work is to build community rather than individual economic success. Thus "the ideal of work is not to be done with it, but to utilize it in giving every member [of the community] an opportunity to develop his faculties."[4] Work is for the Amish an ethical matter, both a means and an end. It is "the fabric of life. [The Amish do] not hurry through the work to be free for the really important things in life. The work [is] the important thing in life."[5]

In order to have a viable community the Amish must provide meaningful work for all members, young and old, male and female, able bodied and disabled. Although farming is the primary small family business of the Amish in Lancaster County, not all members of the community can farm; there is simply not enough land to go around. At the same time, in order to maintain separateness from the world the Amish must rely on their own community for a wide variety of goods and services. As a result, small shops manufacturing items necessary for the ongoing material life of the Amish community dot the Lancaster County countryside, selling such things as furniture, carriages and harness, batteries, farm equipment, dry goods, rugs, book bindings, and Sunday suits (see Color Plate #10).

The small shop network enables most members of the community to engage in meaningful work without leaving the area and keeps alive many of the craft traditions that have been part of the everyday life and values of the Amish for generations. It also allows the Amish a great degree of control and freedom in the area of technological choice, which in turn allows them to remain relatively self-reliant and separate from the world around them. Small shops manufacture quality products that efficiently meet the needs of a "plain" lifestyle in the late twentieth century.

*In accordance with the wishes of the Amish craftsworkers who participated in this exhibition, no mention will be made of individuals or the names and locations of their shops.

CULTURAL ATLAS OF
LANCASTER COUNTY AMISH SHOPS

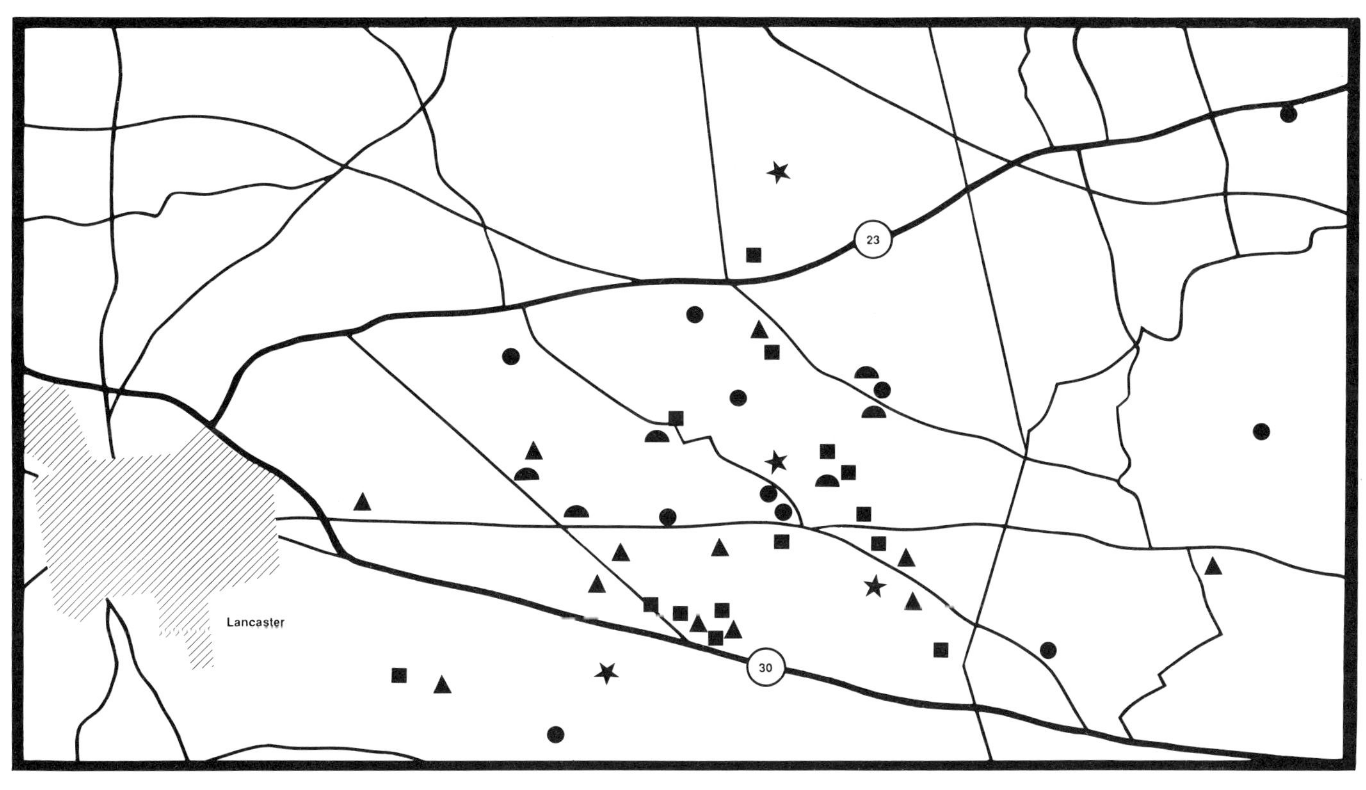

The Amish publish the *Old Order Shop and Service Directory* which lists over four hundred shops making products for plain people. The introduction to the directory states explicitly that these shops exist to "serve" the community through high quality workmanship: "Behind every product is a man or woman who has rendered energy to somewhat shape and form, to achieve to perfect sometime in the course of a lifetime, something that is useful to his fellow consumer."[6] The directory makes clear that the rise of small shops emerges from the importance of making community-based choices about technology: "The American trend, to specialize in one product, to create mass production, to get bigger and greater seemingly has no end, but in Old Order (Amish) culture it has."[7]

The shop directory traces the rise of these shops through a three-phase response to those American technological changes that the Amish found unnecessary and inapplicable to their lives. First, in the 1920s when the automobile replaced the horse and buggy, the Amish began to build their own carriages and buggies. Then, in the 1930s as farm tractors generally replaced horse power, the Amish needed to repair and build their own horse-drawn farm machinery. The third phase of the Amish response came after 1970 and provided a wide range of products that were no longer readily available, such as modern, gas powered farm equipment geared down to be drawn efficiently by horses and gas lamps which generate as bright a light as electric bulbs. Most shops are family businesses which are kept small in order to maintain close personal relations between workers and to allow personal control over the work at hand. Their size also allows for flexibility when other family and community activities interrupt the daily work schedule. Businesses are not simply economic structures, but structures of social and ethical values as well.

No particular piece of technology is perceived as inherently evil by the Amish. Technological choice is based on what is best for the maintenance of a plain and humble lifestyle. It is not any particular tool in and of itself that is suspect. Rather, anything that might break up the community, or threaten members' ability to focus on their lives as disciples of Christ may be rejected. Some technological "improvements" may increase the pace of work and yield greater financial profit and efficiency; however, if there is no time left for visiting and other community activities, or satisfaction in the work at hand, that "improvement" is not likely to be accepted by the community. Moreover, from their point of view it may not be seen as an "improvement."

Although their technological choices may entail selections of items no longer manufactured and used by mainstream American culture, such as horse-drawn carriages and farm equipment, the Amish do not live in the past. Rather, for the Amish the past is alive in the present because it offers technological choices that solve current problems. Their range of available solutions to everyday work problems is much broader than that of the person who must keep up with the latest styles. Amish farms and shops successfully use a variety of energy sources, from human, through horse, diesel, and air power, which match the demands of the problem at hand, and help sustain both the family businesses and the larger community. It is, in part, this flexibility, ingenuity, and ethical commitment that enables small Amish farms and businesses to survive while many larger farms and businesses throughout the country are in default.

Through their small shop network the Amish do remain self-reliant, but they are by no means isolated from the modern world. Although they are self-sufficient in their religious life, socialization patterns, and in most cases in their educational institutions,[8] they are not economically self-sufficient. Milk, hogs, and other farm products, for example, are sold to outside, urban markets, and many supplies are purchased there. The Amish also rely on outside medical services, though their expenses are covered through Amish Aid, a community-based form of insurance.

Two types of craftswork can illustrate the small shop network of the Lancaster County Amish: that devoted to transportation, in this case carriage making; and that devoted to clothing, specifically the manufacture of men's Sunday suits. The Amish carriage is the result of a number of diverse tasks performed in many different shops of various sizes. Sunday suits are the product

Left:
Testimony to the successful blending of beauty and utility, a completed Amish carriage stands in front of the assembly and restoration shop. Lancaster County, 1988.

Above:
The finished carriage, a product of the combined skills of craftworkers in a network of small shops, displays the plain style and careful workmanship that is characteristic of the Amish community. Lancaster County, 1988.

of one or two couples, each of whom makes the complete suit. Carriage construction is primarily young men's work, whereas the making of Sunday suits provides work for women, and sometimes couples, whose children are grown and have families of their own.

The Carriage

The horse-drawn carriage is the primary mode of transportation for the Old Order Amish. What may at first glance seem to be a quaint and simple mode of transportation from out of the past is actually a complex piece of machinery specially designed for short distance travel. Each settlement has its own carriage construction style. The Lancaster County carriage is gray topped with straight sides, an enclosed front, and sliding doors painted black. There are a few shops in Lancaster County that assemble carriages, but rarely does any one shop make the entire vehicle. As many as twelve different full-time occupations combine to create

a carriage. One carriage maker explained that he could establish a business that made each part, but it would require a building acres in size, and it would also defeat the role and purpose of work in the community and take the fun out of it. Not only would insurance and employee benefits become complicated, but there would be little face-to-face communication between employees; managers and workers would be separated. Dividing the work among a number of small shops keeps work in its proper place and perspective in serving the needs of the larger community.

Some shops make only wheel spokes and rims. After air drying for a year, hickory rims are cut, steamed, bent in a hydraulic press, and stacked in a drying room. Spoke material is also cut to size; then the spokes are turned three at a time on an air powered pattern lathe. Like many of the shops that make carriage parts, the spoke and rim shops are usually family businesses that provide work for two to

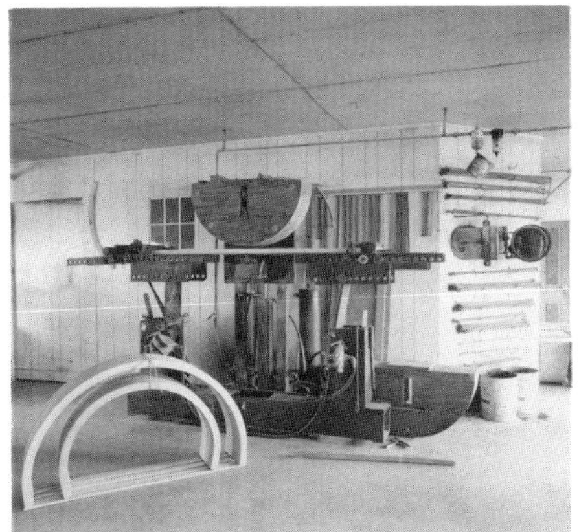

five people. Sons apprentice to their fathers in anticipation of taking over the business when they begin their own families. There is a great demand for rims for all sorts of carriages and wagons, and often the shop will make these items for the burgeoning wagon restoration business. In order to meet the demand, most Amish shops are fully equipped with power tools, which usually run on air power generated by a diesel engine.

Another small shop specializes in bending wood. Here a father, his son, and another community member make hickory shafts, two of which extend from the carriage frame to either side of the horse, where parts of the harness are attached. These shafts are cut on a table saw, but are bent and braced in an early-twentieth-century belt-driven press after they have been steamed in a wood-fired steam box. Manufacture of shafts is complicated by the fact that they are bent in two different directions in order to fit the carriage at one end and the horse at the other. Wood bending requires great ingenuity in the construction of clamps to hold the wood in place after it is steamed. New clamps, usually hydraulically powered, must be made for each design produced. In addition to bending carriage shafts, this shop also bends such things as hay forks, walking canes, antique car fenders, and chair backs. Some of these are for local craftsworker and community consumption, and others are made for larger furniture companies or those who sell to the tourist trade.

There is another shop in the community that specializes in making axles, not only for Amish carriages but for antique carriages and wagons as well. The shop is owned and operated by one person with the help of one employee. The owner is busy enough to hire more workers but would rather help someone else start a separate business in order to keep his own work under control. The axles are made of high-quality steel that is carefully turned on a lathe, bent, trued with an axle gauge of the shop owner's design, and fitted to self-lubricating bearings especially chosen for cool, low-friction wear at slow speeds. Five-leaf, elliptic, spring-steel springs are made at another two-man shop, and hydraulic brakes at another. Spokes, rims, brakes, axles, springs, and shafts are all delivered to another shop where the entire carriage is assembled.

The carriage body, called a "pot," is made at yet another shop owned and operated by a father and his son. Most pots in Lancaster County are currently constructed of six layers of fiberglass in a stainless steel mold. This shop makes pots for almost all the carriages in the county. Pots are delivered to the same shop that assembles the carriage wheels and running gear. The assembly shop is one of the larger operations and has four full-time and three part-time employees. The work crew makes the frames for the roof and sides of the carriage, called carriage "bows," and attaches them to the fiberglas pot. The same shop also assembles wheels and the undercarriage, sews and installs a gray canvas cover over the bows, and makes the carriage's sliding doors and front window frames.

Above:
The hydraulic press (left side of table top) was designed and made to bend a variety of front and rear carriage axles. Curviture is checked against a wooden pattern, the "axle bed" (sitting on right side of table top). Lancaster County, 1988.

Right:
Wooden "bows" used to frame the sides and roof of the carriage, made at one shop, and the fiberglass bodies, or "pots," made at another shop, are joined here at a third shop where the entire carriage is assembled. Lancaster County, 1988.

Carriage headlights, a combination of light and reflector, are specially designed and made at another Amish shop that is also widely known for its expert coach and wagon restoration work. Another Amish shop does nothing but make harnesses, again not only for Amish carriages but for equestrians around the country. Although the primary responsibility of these carriage makers is to the local plain community, almost every shop is well known for its expert craftsmanship and serves outsiders as well.

Right:
Amish carriage lamp
(checklist #111)

Below:
Parts for Amish carriage
lamp (checklist #112
through #120)

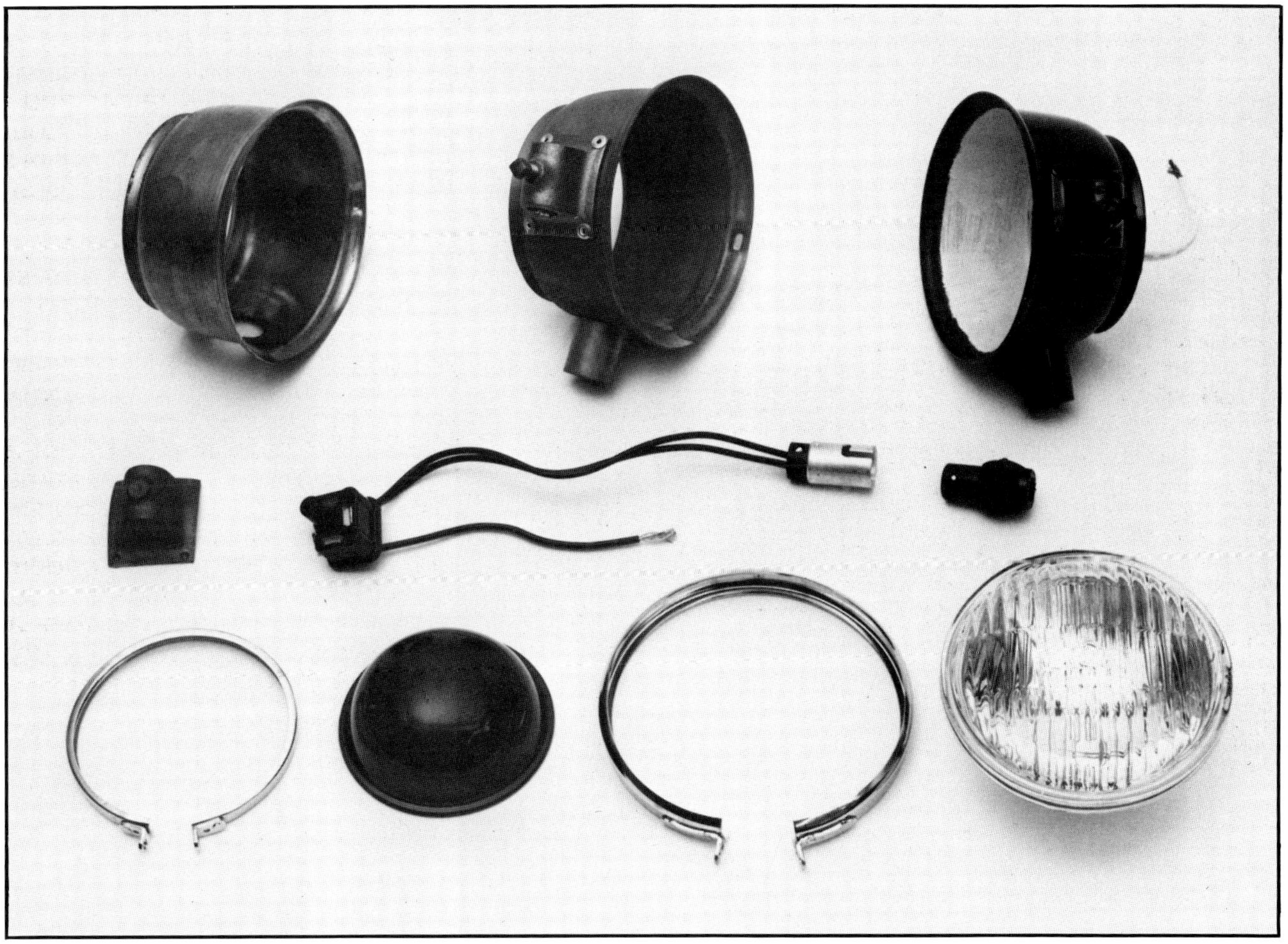

The Sunday Suit

Unlike carriage making, the manufacture of men's Sunday suits is a business that serves only members of the immediate community and one in which one or two people make the entire product. Everyday clothes are made by women in each family, but because the manufacture of men's Sunday suits is a task requiring a great deal of time and specialized skills, there are only a few suit makers in Lancaster County. Such work is usually done by older women and men, one of whose children has taken over management of the family farm. The couple usually lives and works in the *Grossdaadi Haus*, or "grandfather house," which is attached to the main house where their son's family lives. The suit-making business provides work for this couple and a service to the community, fulfilling the Amish tenet that no member of the community be without *meaningful* work.

The Amish man's suit consists of a pair of button-front ("broadfall") pants, a vest, and a suit jacket called a *mutze*. Black suit material, purchased in New York or Philadelphia, is usually synthetic. While plain in color, the material is often subtly textured, and although plain in design, the workmanship is detailed, painstaking, and impeccable. As with carriage design, each Amish settlement has made its own choices about particular details, and these are well outlined in Stephen Scott's book, *Why Do They Dress That Way?*[9]

In Lancaster County, broadfall pants, fully lined with a dacron-cotton material, are made with two front pockets and a watch pocket, as well as buttons for the x-type, elastic suspenders, which can be purchased at any clothing store.

Left:
Amish women's dress (checklist #128) and apron (checklist #127)

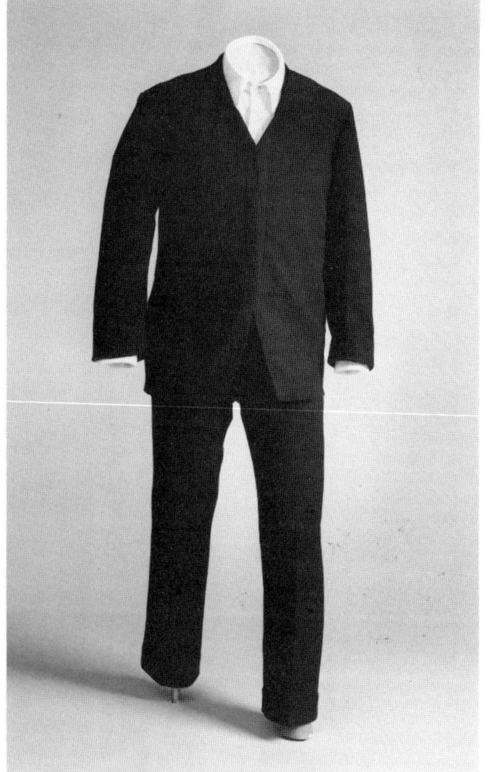

Left:
Amish men's Sunday suit (checklist #131 through #135)

Above:
Southern and western light pours into an Amish suit maker's workspace, illuminating the fabric-cutting and pinning table on the left, and irons, a battery-powered sewing machine, and gas lamp in front of the window on the right. Lancaster County, 1988.

The vest is lined with satin and has one inside pocket. The mutze has a complicated back design, a rounded collar lined with a stiffening material, and a layer of horsehair between the outside suit fabric and its satin lining. Both it and the vest are fastened with hooks and eyes. A great deal of time and care are required to make a Sunday suit, and patterns must be made for males of all ages and sizes.

As in local carriage shops, a variety of energy sources supply power to the tools used for making suits. Sewing may be done partly by hand and partly with an antique treadle sewing machine converted to battery power. The battery is recharged by the same diesel engine that powers the dairy's milking machines. Material is pressed with irons heated on a gas powered double burner. The suit-making business is not unlike the farming business: both are small family enterprises that make use of the broad range of technological choices available within the bounds of Amish work ethics.

The small shops of Lancaster County contribute to the stability and growth of the Amish community in a number of ways. They provide work for non-farming members of the community. That work, which is a crucial way of enacting a belief in the importance of humility and stewardship, forges family and community strength and self-reliance, religiously, socially, and economically. Because work is one of the most constant modes of worship, Amish shops are also places where objects that are plain in design demand devotion to detailed workmanship. The everyday objects made in these shops speak eloquently of the personal care, dexterity, and responsibility entailed in their making.

Notes

1. Sandra Lee Cronk, *"Gelassenheit:* The Rites of the Redemptive Process in Old Order Amish and Old Order Mennonite Communities" (Ph.D. diss., University of Chicago Divinity School, 1977), p. 10.

2. Ibid., p. 10.

3. John A. Hostetler, *Amish Society* (Baltimore: Johns Hopkins University Press, 1968), p. 9.

4. Ibid., p. 381.

5. Cronk, *"Gelassenheit,"* p.57.

6. Joseph F. Beiler, *Old Order Shop and Service Directory* (Gordonville, Pa.: n.p., 1977), p. i.

7. Ibid.

8. Hostetler, *Amish Society*, p. 15.

9. Stephen Scott, *Why Do They Dress That Way?* (Intercourse, Pa.: Good Books, 1986), pp. 122-5.

Suggested Reading

Bachman, Calvin George. *The Old Order Amish of Lancaster County*. Publications of the Pennsylvania German Society, Vol. 60. Lancaster, Pa.: Franklin and Marshall College Library, 1956.

Brown, Waln K. "The Pennsylvania Dutch Carriage Trade." *Pennsylvania Folklife* 22, no. 3 (1973):22-36.

Fisher, Gideon. *Farm Life and Its Changes*. Gordonville, Pa.: Pequea Publishers, 1978.

Gallagher, Thomas E. "Clinging to the Past or Preparing for the Future? The Structure of Selective Modernization Among the Old Order Amish of Lancaster County." Ph.D. diss., Temple University, 1981.

Kollmorgen, Walter M. *Culture of a Contemporary Rural Community: The Old Order Amish of Lancaster County, Pennsylvania*. Rural Life Studies, Vol. 4. Washington, D.C.: U.S. Department of Agriculture, U.S. Bureau of Agricultural Economics, 1942.

Redfield, Robert. *The Little Community* Chicago: University of Chicago Press, 1955.

Scott, Stephen. *Plain Buggies*. Intercourse, Pa.: Good Books, 1981.

Sturt, George. *The Wheelwright's Shop*. New York: Cambridge University Press, 1976.

PYSANKY:
Craftsmanship, Ritual Meaning, and Ethnic Identity

Doris J. Dyen

For Ukrainian Americans of Carnegie, Pennsylvania, *pysanky* ("egg-writing") is a ritual experience that integrates religion, ethnicity, and artistic expression. It is a craft that contributes to the community members' ability to maintain their identity as Ukrainians, both among themselves and to outsiders.

Carnegie, named for steelmaker Andrew Carnegie, lies about five miles southwest of Pittsburgh. Ukrainians began to immigrate to Carnegie in the late nineteenth and early twentieth centuries along with other eastern Europeans, to work as coal miners, railroaders, factory hands and millworkers. Most were from the Lemko region in western Ukraine which was then part of the Austrian province of Galicia. Geographically close to Slovakia and Poland —and politically connected to them at various times in history—the Lemko region nevertheless always remained tied to Ukraine as a whole in language and heritage.

Ukrainian immigrant settlements arose in several parts of the Pittsburgh area, but the Ukrainian community in Carnegie has remained the largest and most cohesive. Because many families have been living there for three generations, the community is now a complex kinship network of extended families related by blood and marriage, resembling an old-country village.

Ukrainian cultural activity in Carnegie centers on the Ukrainian Club and the churches. In addition to Holy Trinity Ukrainian Catholic Church, there is SS. Peter and Paul Ukrainian Orthodox Church, with its own active cultural organization, the Ukrainian Orthodox League. This church and the League have taken the lead in encouraging the perpetuation of Ukrainian religious practices, language, performing arts, crafts, food traditions, and other customs.

Pysanky is one of the customs associated with the Easter holiday, not only in Ukraine but throughout eastern Europe. Like many such customs, it was a pre-Christian practice into which Christian symbolism was later introduced. Thus while some of the motifs refer to the springtime reawakening of the natural world after winter dormancy (the sun, plants such as pussy willow and wheat, animals such as chickens for fertility) and to the continuity of life (fir-tree branch, the "everlasting line"); others refer specifically to the death and resurrection of Christ (the cross, the triangle for the Trinity). Decorated eggs traditionally were given as gifts, and sometimes placed at key points near the house, barn, and fields to bring prosperity for the coming year and to ward off evil.

Each cultural area in eastern Europe has its own styles and techniques of egg decoration. Decorative styles range from floral or animal shapes to geometric designs. A common technique is known as the wax-resist method; other techniques include filing and etching. There are many regional styles within Ukraine alone, including three major styles from the western regions: Boyko, Hutsul, and Lemko. In parts of the western and central regions, egg-writers utilize the multi-color, wax-resist method: successive layers of wax are applied to the raw egg in a writing or sketching motion as it goes through several dye-baths. After that, the wax is heated and rubbed off, leaving the intricate design visible (see Color Plate #11).

In the Lemko style which Ukrainian immigrants brought to Carnegie, designs are placed on a raw or hard-boiled, white egg. Using a dish of beeswax heated at the stove or over a candle and a stylus made from a wooden stick with a pin stuck in it, the egg-writer creates floral designs, sunbursts, and other motifs with short, quick strokes in the "drop-pull" method. This method leaves the wax in tear-drop-shaped lines on the egg. After the design has been applied, the egg is put into one dye-bath, then the wax is heated and rubbed off. An alternative method now is to dye the egg first— or to leave it white throughout—and apply clear or tinted wax which is then allowed to remain on the egg as part of the finished design.

Until the 1960s egg-writing among Ukrainians in Carnegie was practiced only in the home, as part of the traditional preparation for Easter. Egg-writing was done during the few days preceding Easter by the women of the household, late at night after the evening meal had been completed and the younger children put to bed. This home-centered tradition still continues in the community. Families place their finished eggs in a basket along with the holiday foods to be eaten on Easter Sunday, cover the basket with an embroidered cloth, and take it to church to be blessed by the priest in a special ceremony, either on Holy Saturday evening or on Easter morning. Each family then gives the priest a decorated egg as a token of respect (see Color Plate #13).

Below:
Steve and Beverly Kapeluck create *pysanky* for personal and ritual use in their home where they also display their prized collection of Ukrainian hand-written eggs. Carnegie, 1987.

Throughout Easter Sunday the eggs are exchanged as gifts among relatives and close friends. Eggs with certain colors or motifs are considered appropriate for certain family members or social situations: eggs with a cross motif or other religious symbol for the priest, white-background eggs (symbolizing purity) for very young children and eggs with roosters (symbolizing fertility) on them for the wife in a newly married couple. Families set aside certain areas in their homes to display eggs that have been received as gifts along with family photographs and memorabilia, folk-art objects such as carvings from Ukraine, and religious items such as icons, palm leaves, and pussy willow branches.

In 1966, Beverly Kapeluck suggested that the Carnegie chapter of the Ukrainian Orthodox League sponsor classes in egg-writing at SS. Peter and Paul Church. A woman of central Ukrainian descent from Minneapolis, Mrs. Kapeluck had married Carnegie native Stephen Kapeluck a few years before. She had learned from her mother and other relatives pysanky in the multi-colored, geometric, wax-resist style typical of the Hutsul region of western Ukraine (see Color Plate #12). As the teacher for the League's classes, she began to impart this style to Carnegie residents. Over the years this style has become widely practiced in Carnegie, although several people still know the Lemko tradition and a few—such as Steve Kapeluck and his son Michael—continue to make pysanky in that western Ukrainian style.

The egg-writing classes have evolved into an organized part of the Ukrainian Orthodox League's yearly fundraising effort for the church itself and for scholarships and activities that highlight the Ukrainian cultural heritage. Beginning in January right after Orthodox Christmas and continuing until late spring, egg-writing sessions are held in the church hall each Friday night, producing about 1,000 pysanky per year. The sessions are attended by 10-15 egg-writers ranging in age from children six or seven years old to women and men in their seventies. The group varies from week to week and from year to year. In any one year about 35-40 people are involved. Over the years, about 100 people have participated; many have been coming ever since the classes started.

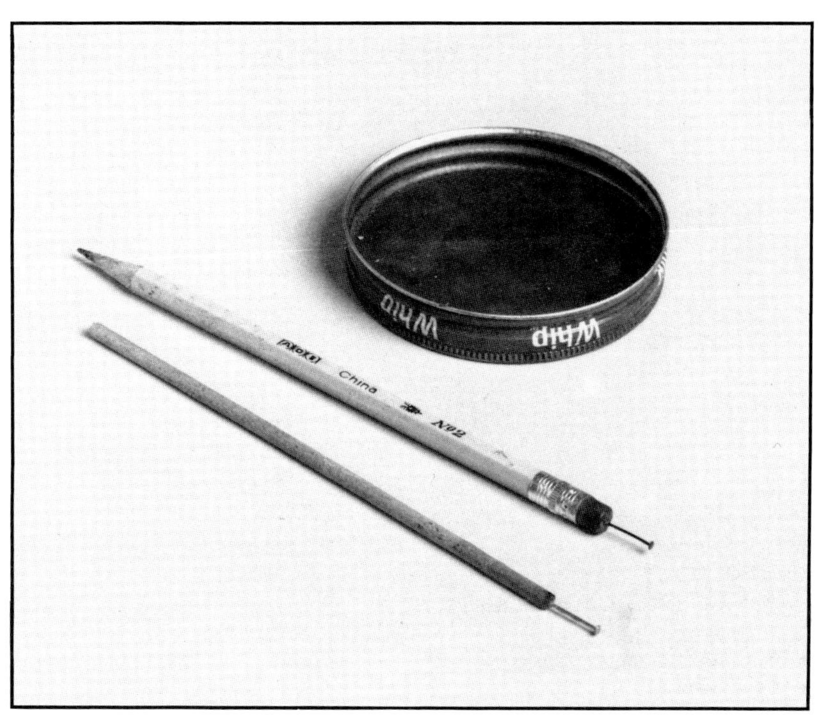

Above:
Kistky (styluses; checklist #148 and #149) and beeswax (checklist #153) used in the Lemko tradition of producing *pysanky*

Left:
Kistky (checklist #150, #151 and #152) and beeswax (checklist #154, #155, #156, #157 and #158) used in the Hutsul and other wax-resist traditions of producing *pysanky*

Above:
The electric stylus is a modern adaptation which has streamlined the process of *pysanky*. Carnegie, 1987.

Above:
After applying wax with the stylus, Pearl Makar dips the egg into a dye bath. Color adheres where there is no wax. Carnegie, 1987.

Because so many of the participants are related to each other, the atmosphere is like that of a family gathering, good-natured teasing combined with hearty approval and encouragement. The Friday night sessions blend informal instruction with artistic creation. Each egg-writer works on designs according to his or her abilities and interests, guided by Beverly Kapeluck or one of the other senior writers. Some use the traditional *kistka*, a wooden stylus with a small copper funnel attached to it. The kistka is heated in a candle flame, then dipped onto a small block of beeswax. Other writers use a modernized version that has a plastic handle substituted for the wooden one, or employ an electric stylus that provides a continuous flow of heated wax and eliminates the need for a candle. Tinted beeswax is often used as well to make it easier to see the lines as they are drawn on the egg.

Many writers work on intricate designs that may take hours to complete. Some take such eggs home and finish them during the week, preferring to do the most complicated sections in quieter surroundings that allow them to concentrate better. Other writers work on "community eggs" that have been "outlined" or started by one writer and are then given to others to complete as a way of streamlining the process. One woman prepares for each week's session by outlining several eggs to be finished this way.

Children and other beginning egg-writers usually start on the eight-pointed star, a traditional motif that is considered easy to master. This motif teaches the writer the basic techniques of the geometric, multi-color method: how to "quarter" (section) the egg's surface and how to build up a design through various dye stages. Writers go on to learn more complicated designs, first by completing outlined eggs, then by initiating designs themselves. Although quickness of hand is important because of the quantity of eggs needed for the fundraisers, the writers are careful to point out that speed alone does not guarantee the quality or beauty of a finished egg.

The types of designs used in these church-centered egg-writing sessions have evolved through several stages since the 1960s. The first stage, building upon the community's knowledge of egg-writing in the Lemko style, was the introduction of the Hutsul style by Beverly Kapeluck. A second stage was reached when egg-writers began to seek out new motifs to use, learning from books published by Ukrainian groups elsewhere in the United States and creating their own designs and techniques. Often they combined motifs from several regions of Ukraine on one egg to give a desired artistic effect. Recently, though, there has been a movement back towards a more purist approach. Writers have been adopting the principle that an egg destined for the public sale should not mix regional styles; any one egg should incorporate motifs, techniques, and colors from only one Ukrainian region. At the same time, members have continued to explore new techniques and create new designs with eggs they mean to keep for private display. On these eggs, which may be from birds other than chickens including ducks, geese, and even ostriches, non-traditional motifs appear, such as the poppy (the Ukrainian national flower), human likenesses—dance figures in Ukrainian costume, for example, and gold-leafed icons (see Color Plate #14).

There are now several events each year where the pysanky made in the Carnegie community's egg-writing sessions are sold or displayed. These events are not only fundraisers but public rituals of ethnicity, counterpart in some ways to the private, religious rituals discussed earlier. Both types of ritual reinforce a sense of community identity among the Carnegie Ukrainians themselves and, by extension, among other Ukrainians in the region and beyond.

The annual egg sale at SS. Peter and Paul is the main event hosted entirely by the Carnegie Ukrainian Orthodox community. The sale always occurs on Palm Sunday—not the Orthodox Palm Sunday but the holiday as determined by the Roman Catholic Church's calendar, which the Orthodox in Carnegie refer to as "American Palm Sunday." This scheduling accomplishes three things: it makes the public connection of pysanky with the Easter religious holiday; it affords the best chance of a good turnout as most groups celebrate Easter according to the Catholic/Protestant calendar; and it allows Carnegie's Orthodox Ukrainians to separate this public ritual of ethnicity from their private religious celebration of Holy Week itself, except in rare years (such as 1987) when both observances coincide.

The sale is a popular regional ethnic event. Ukrainians from other nearby communities come every year along with others of Eastern European descent and many who are interested in the eggs as art rather than ethnic or religious objects. Most of the eggs are usually sold within the first two hours of the event, which begins Sunday morning and lasts until mid-afternoon.

The egg sale is held in the large social room upstairs in the church hall (next door to the church itself). On one side of the room are long tables with the eggs arranged for easy viewing. There is one table nearby for egg-writing demonstrations. Across the room is a display of Ukrainian religious and ethnic objects: display eggs, including Michael Kapeluck's exhibit of eggs from all the regions of Ukraine, a wooden model of the Carnegie church, figurines in Ukrainian regional costumes, pussy willow branches and palm leaves, and a basket containing Easter candles, *paska* bread (shellacked for display) and a *servetka*, an embroidered cloth. On the lower floor of the church hall, *pirohi* and other Ukrainian foods are sold. One can also buy whole Easter paska breads to take home. All those assisting with the sale wear some article of Ukrainian clothing, usually an embroidered shirt or blouse.

The Ukrainian Festival at the University of Pittsburgh is one of several ethnic festivals held at the Cathedral of Learning (a classroom and office building). For this two-day event, the Ukrainians of Carnegie work together with those from other Pittsburgh-area neighborhoods, elsewhere in Pennsylvania, the northeastern U.S., and even Canada. The Carnegie Ukrainians help with preparing and selling Ukrainian foods; their performing ensemble takes part and they have an egg-writing demonstration and display as one of the exhibits.

Participation in the Pittsburgh Folk Festival is similar to that in the Ukrainian Festival, but here, the Ukrainians are only one of several dozen different ethnic groups included. In 1988, when the Folk Festival featured Ukrainians as one of its highlighted nationalities, the Carnegie Ukrainian Orthodox League along with the Western Pennsylvania League of Ukrainian Catholics took the lead in putting together a large display and demonstration of Ukrainian crafts. Egg-writing figured prominently along with embroidery and paska-making. Because 1988 was also the millennium of the introduction of Christianity to Ukraine, the group decided to emphasize Easter rituals and customs as the theme for their presentation of Ukrainian heritage.

In addition to these regional events, there are nationwide occasions that focus on pysanky as part of Ukrainian culture. One example is the egg contests sponsored by the Ukrainian Orthodox League to foster interest in and perpetuation of the art. Several members of the Carnegie community have won top prizes in these competitions. "Contest eggs," as these entries are called, usually are not sold, but remain in the private collections of the egg-writers for display at home.

As at the Palm Sunday sale, all those from the Carnegie community who participate in the various ethnic festival events are encouraged, both by others in the community and by the organizers of the events, to dress in Ukrainian clothing to "look the part." Many feel it important to maintain a public image of authenticity in other ways as well. For example, the Carnegie group considers it inappropriate to use an electric kistka in public egg-writing demonstrations. Instead, all egg-writers use the wooden-handled kistka with the beeswax block and candle-flame and focus on what they feel are the most traditional motifs.

The style of egg-writing which developed in the church-centered classes to prepare for public "ethnic" events emphasizes strict adherence to traditional techniques and motifs. This emphasis would seem to conflict strongly with the private, home-centered style which cherishes experimentation, yet they are actually complementary. Each style reinforces the other and enables the other to exist. The egg sale, the festival egg-writing demonstrations, and the pysanky contests become public rituals of ethnicity because they have evolved customs— modes of dress, tools and techniques of presentation, sanctioned symbolic motifs—that intensify the participants' sense of group membership and serve a higher purpose: the perpetuation of ethnic identity from one generation to the next.

Suggested Reading

Grobman, Neil R. *Wycinanki and Pysanky: Forms of Religious and Ethnic Art from the Delaware Valley.* Pittsburgh: Pennsylvania Ethnic Heritage Studies Center, University of Pittsburgh, 1981.

Halich, Wasyl. "Ukrainians in Western Pennsylvania." *Western Pennsylvania Historical Magazine* 18 (1935): 139-46.

Kmit, Anne, Loretta Luciow, and Luba Perchyshyn. *Ukrainian Easter Eggs and How We Make Them.* Minneapolis: Harrison, Smith-Lund Press, 1979.

Luciow, Johanna, Anne Kmit, and Loretta Luciow. *Eggs Beautiful: How to Make Ukrainian Easter Eggs.* Minneapolis: Harrison, Smith-Lund Press, 1975.

Newall, Venetia. *An Egg at Easter: A Folklore Study.* Bloomington: Indiana University Press, 1971.

Procko, Bohdan. "Pennsylvania: Focal Point of Ukrainian Immigration." In *The Ethnic Experience in Pennsylvania,* edited by John Bodnar, pp. 216-32. Lewisburg, Pa.: Bucknell University Press, 1973.

Surmach, Yaroslava. *Ukrainian Easter Eggs.* New York: Surma, 1955.

Tkachuk, Mary, Marie Kishchuk, and Alice Nicholaichuk. *Pysanka: Icon of the Universe.* Saskatoon, Saskatchewan, Canada: Ukrainian Museum of Canada, 1977.

"THEY KNOW THE RULE FOR WHAT WILL MAKE IT PRETTY": Hmong Material Traditions in Translation*

Sally Peterson

Craft fair visitors marvel as spiralling geometries swirl upon the cloth, held still by the skill of needle and thread. Elephant's Foot, Crab's Hand, Buffalo Heads and Snail Horns—the ancient designs of clan and kingdom—shape the contours of place mats, eyeglass cases, pincushions. Hmong women in the United States practice their timeless traditions of embroidery, appliqué, and batik, translating form and color to please an alien audience.

Far from the Laotian forests of greening bamboo, a Hmong assembly line worker gathers plastic strapping from a factory floor; later he will weave the strips into baskets for collecting garden vegetables, packing clothing, and storing needlework. The brightly colored baskets circulate within the Hmong community, fulfilling traditional requirements for portability and storage capacity. The Hmong basketmaker has effected a material translation, substituting petroleum-based fiber for the natural resource of bamboo.

The material traditions of a community—the fashioning of objects and the knowledge and tools necessary for their making—carry meanings that often lie below the level of language yet reverberate through every facet of life. Items of material culture embody shared philosophies, plans of action, and fundamental knowledge about the ways of the world. The Hmong from Laos came to the United States with a broad repertoire of material traditions. The need to gain competence in the industrial and educational technocracies of North America, however, has convinced many Hmong to lay aside their knives and needles. Others have responded to new markets and materials by increasing their production of traditional objects. As a result, no tradition has emerged unchanged from the crucible of resettlement.

Despite transformations of meaning, market, method, and materials, essential principles of aesthetic judgment continue to dictate the step-by-step choices made by artists as they create. Though rarely articulated in words by members of the Hmong community, these principles are observable, logical, and persistent. From the most sacred embellishment on a spirit altar to the most mundane of tourist items, certain conventions of form and space order the structure of material manufacture. This is evident in the age-old tradition of *paj ntaub* (pronounced pa ndau, and translated as "flower cloth") and is echoed in the recent innovation of plastic-strap basketry.

A Hmong woman who stitches the intricate paj ntaub relies on her eye as the primary measuring tool for establishing the principle of exact *symmetry*. Intensifying the design through contrasting colors, related in a system of *complementarity*, she manipulates both pattern shape and hue to create a visible *balance* between foreground and background. The contours of the design field are defined with an inexorable *precision* that reveals the artist's skills with a needle. A needleworker wins deserving admiration when she draws upon individual *creativity* to combine and recombine ancient designs that have been handed down from generation to generation. Hmong women strive for the successful expression of these aesthetic principles. The goal is nothing short of perfection.

* The quotation is from an interview with PaVue Thao, January 16, 1986, in Merced, California.

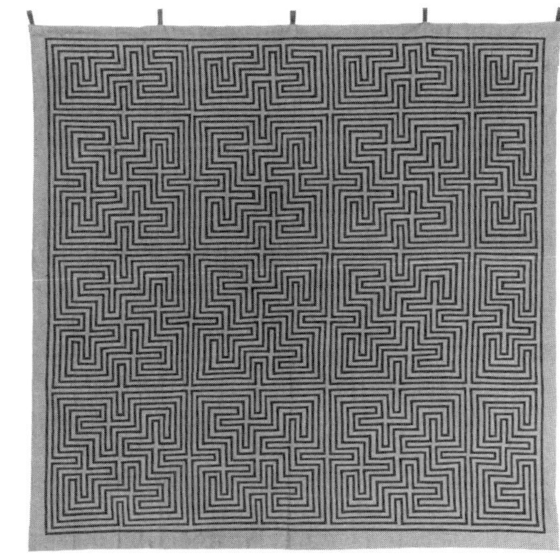

Hmong men in Laos practice many crafts requiring skill and dexterity. While a number of artists specialize in smithing iron and silver, nearly all men know basic woodworking and basketmaking skills.[1] Most baskets are woven from bamboo, an abundant resource in the highlands of Southeast Asia. Woven bamboo containers are used for harvesting, winnowing, cooking, storing food, and housing animals. Plaited bamboo is also fashioned into several varieties of hunting traps. Valued primarily for their function, baskets are not overtly considered an art form by the Hmong. Yet a finely woven basket excites admiration, and the Hmong count many complex design techniques in their weaving repertoire. The principles governing the weaving of bamboo parallel those defining the aesthetics of paj ntaub, including the emphasis on symmetry, balance, precision, and creativity. The substitution of plastic coiled strapping for bamboo has heightened the importance of color combinations, and experiments in complementarity and the interplay of bold and subtle contrasts mark the creative skill of contemporary basketmakers.

Observable consistencies in the traditional expressive arts of the Hmong both identify cultural characteristics and suggest cultural values. Even so, outlining aesthetic principles can only imply the meanings these arts hold for the people who practice them. The state of Hmong contemporary and traditional art is a direct outcome of the cataclysmic events of recent Hmong history. Neither the sacrifices of tradition—nor the sacrifices made *for* tradition—can be understood outside of this historical context.

The Hmong, one of the largest ethnic minorities in Asia, reside primarily in the southeastern highlands, a territory encompassed by the national boundaries of China, Vietnam, Laos, Thailand, and Burma. Tracing their origin to northern China, the Hmong relate histories of continuous southbound migrations, due to political and economic exigencies. Both oral testimonies of Hmong individuals and written accounts of Chinese historians attest to the will of the Hmong to retain their identity as a separate people and to resist assimilation into the majority culture of China.[2]

Within their collective identity as "Hmong," the Hmong people acknowledge many subdivisions; differences in language, custom, ritual, dress, and geographic location distinguish subgroups from each other. Most of these groups are outwardly identified by prominent colors in clothing or features of dress so that members of different divisions refer to each other as White Hmong, Green Hmong, Striped Hmong, or Black Hmong, for example.

Nearly two centuries ago a large number of Hmong established settlements in the northern mountains of Laos. Here their numbers grew to the hundreds of thousands as they maintained cultural independence while incorporating innovations learned from their Lao neighbors.

The historic upheavals that drew the era of colonialism to a close fostered within most countries of Southeast Asia the development of nationalistic organizations, many of which embraced Marxist philosophy. When Laos gained its independence in 1954, the nationalist government loyal to the crown was immediately forced into confrontation with the communist nationalists—the Pathet Lao. Much of the resulting military conflict took place in territories inhabited by the Hmong. Depending upon circumstance and family affiliation, the Hmong allied themselves with either the communists or the Royalists, but the majority remained loyal to the Kingdom of Laos.

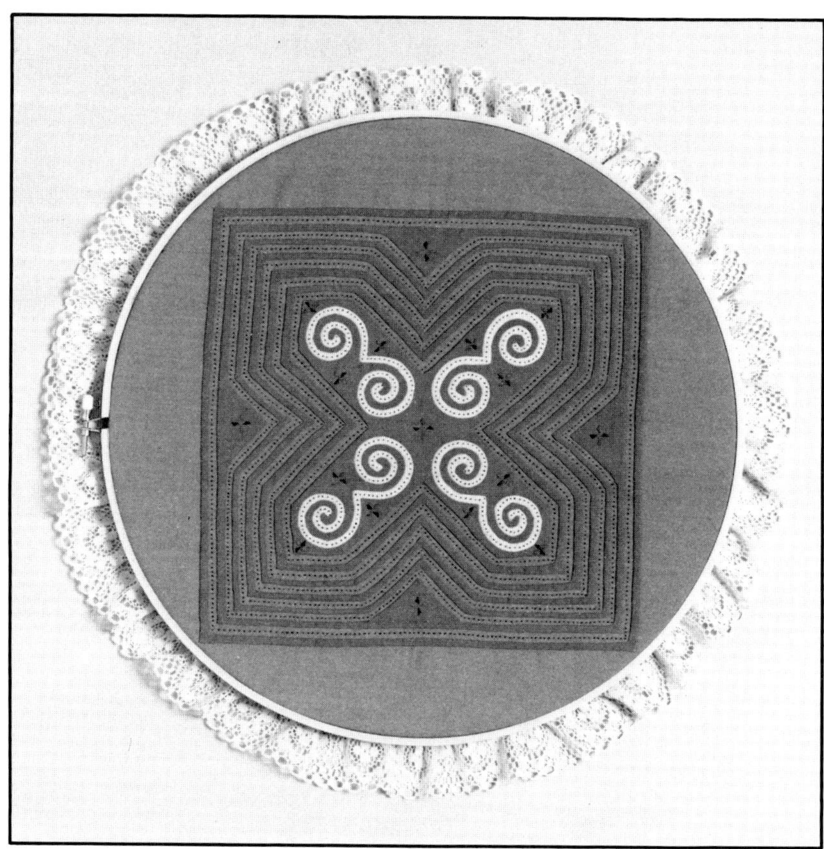

Above:
Paj ntaub ("Protective Cross with Snails" design) by Mao Moua (checklist #171)

When the United States entered the Laotian conflict in the early 1960s, the CIA supervised a little-publicized army recruited largely from the Hmong and other highland populations to war against the Pathet Lao and North Vietnamese forces. This struggle continued for over 15 years. With the withdrawal of U.S. support in 1973 and the subsequent collapse of a coalition government in 1975, those Hmong associated with Royalists and Americans were placed in great jeopardy. Facing fierce reprisals from the triumphant communist forces, over a hundred thousand Hmong fled Laos. Many lost their lives as they risked passage through treacherous jungles, chanced discovery by military patrols, and hazarded the final dangerous crossing of the Mekong River to sanctuary in Thailand.[3]

From Thai refugee camps, thousands of Hmong resettled in France, Australia, Canada, West Germany, and the United States. Estimates of their numbers in North America range from 50,000 to 70,000.[4] The Hmong have established communities from Oregon to Georgia. California alone is home to more than 20,000, and Michigan, Wisconsin, Minnesota, Massachusetts, Rhode Island, Colorado, Texas, Ohio, and Washington also boast large Hmong communities. Philadelphia was one of the first cities to receive resettling Hmong, but since the late 1970s many of these immigrants have moved to Pennsylvania's rural areas or have rejoined relatives in other states.

Fortunately the Hmong have been able to rely on a dynamic system of family and community leadership in facing the inevitable problems adapting to a foreign culture.[5] Confronted with a new language, new occupations, and new systems of education, household management, and transportation, the Hmong turned to their own communal support networks based on systems of reciprocity and family relationships. An extensive system of family groupings called clans, whose lineages trace back as far as six generations, establishes structured relationships with attendant obligations.

Respect and obligation for one's family and clan is a crucial value in Hmong philosophy, reinforced through many practices and beliefs. Although many Hmong in the United States are devout Christians, a number of community members, particularly elders, remain loyal to the religion of their fathers. Usually termed "animism" in the literature of Western culture, Hmong religion recognizes the existence of a spirit world which interacts directly with humans. The spirits of one's ancestors retain a particular importance; each man must shoulder the responsibility of caring for his family's spirits in death as well as in life. Ful-

fillment of obligations to one's ancestors reaps benefits for one's progeny as the spirits watch over and care for the living.[6]

In their Laotian homeland the primary occupation of most Hmong was farming. The yearly agrarian cycle was punctuated with the celebration of the New Year, a festive event which reunited families and communities, affirming old ties and establishing new alliances through marriage. The advent of war diversified traditional occupational pursuits; the roles of soldier and merchant grew more important, and young people increasingly began to take advantage of emerging educational opportunities. Since resettlement few Hmong in the United States have been able to pursue agriculture, relying instead on employment in industry and service occupations. Increasingly, youthful Hmong are earning university degrees and entering professional fields. Despite the changes of the recent past, however, the New Year celebration continues to be the most eagerly anticipated social event of the year as friends and relatives visit each other's communities to share in the festivities.

Although paj ntaub textiles have become the major material tradition through which Hmong culture has been introduced to the American public, the rectangular wall hangings displayed at craft fairs and in galleries differ widely from traditional forms of this needlework. Within Hmong communities, paj ntaub decorates the clothing of men and women, visibly identifying the traditions of the various subgroups. Women in all these subgroups practice several forms of embroidery, with counted cross-stitch ranking as one of the most popular. Various types of appliqué, in which layers of pieced fabric are sewn directly onto a background cloth, are also utilized throughout Hmong culture. White Hmong women from Laos excel at reverse appliqué, a technique relying on the interplay of the backing cloth with the applied fabric. Green Hmong women, in contrast, have mastered the art of batik. They first apply intricate patterns of hot wax to a white cloth; then dye the whole in indigo. Later removal of the wax reveals a complex design set palely against the blue indigo field. Appliquéd strips of red complement the stark contrast of dark blue and white, outlining features of the design.

Paj ntaub traditionally plays an important role in the cycle of life. Baby carriers—gifts from mothers to their daughters—sport symbolic designs which protect the grandchild from evil. Women strive to provide their families with new clothes to celebrate each New Year; wearing layers of paj ntaub not only enhances natural beauty but also announces one's skill to the community. Daughters also receive a trousseau of finely stitched clothes when they marry. Children return the gift of paj ntaub to their parents by providing them with elaborate funeral clothing and pillows. An expression of love, respect, and gratitude, these gifts also ensure the comfort of the elders when they reach the spirit world.

Although the Hmong did not abandon their expressive traditions after the Laotian exodus, refugee camp life and subsequent resettlement have had a considerable impact. Paj ntaub, once reserved for personal adornment and community recognition, now serves a primarily economic function, dependent upon support from consumers outside the Hmong community. New forms of paj ntaub have developed with the advent of refugee status. Left with few economic resources, Hmong women in refugee camps quickly utilized their enforced leisure to adapt traditional designs and techniques to forms valued by Western consumers. As a result, traditional patterns created by the manipulation of geometric shapes are now fashioned into wall hangings, purses, bedspreads, and a host of inexpensive items. Women have experimented with "earth tones" and pastels in response to contemporary trends of Western decor; stitch size has increased as designs are cut to a larger scale and embroidered embellishments have been simplified or have disappeared.

Yet production to a larger scale and for a foreign audience has not always led to simplification. The design field of a traditional Hmong piece rarely exceeds a six-inch square, but challenged by the marketability of large textiles, Hmong women have explored the logical extensions of traditional designs, creating feats of geometric complexity rarely achieved in their traditional forms.

Despite continuous adjustment and experimentation, paj ntaub offered to consumers outside the Hmong community displays familiar aesthetic principles. Precision cutting and invisible stitching remain trademarks of Hmong handiwork, and symmetry and balance still dictate the placement of designs. Though Hmong women often remark on the lack of clarity resulting from the absence of bright color

Below:
Detail of *paj ntaub* ("story cloth") illustrating the escape of the Hmong to the refugee camps in Thailand by Youa Vang (checklist #170)

contrasts, they nonetheless carefully combine "American" hues according to principles of complementarity.

Men in refugee camps join with women in the production of an entirely new form of paj ntaub, commonly termed "story cloths" (see Color Plate #15). The men pencil onto cloth pictorial details of folktales, scenes of everyday life, and panoramas depicting the flora and fauna of the Laotian highlands. Spectactular historic epics record painfully accurate testimonies of the recent war and dispersal. Women complete the drawn depictions with a time-consuming satin or chainstitch embroidery. The resulting forms provide curious consumers with insights about the culture of the artists whose work they purchase.

Hmong women in the United States continue to fabricate and sell their needlework. Occasionally pieces find their way into Hmong homes, where their primarily economic function fades as they are reincorporated into Hmong private life. Hmong families often choose to decorate sofas, beds, and chairs with paj ntaub pillows, or brighten a coffee table with an intricately stitched table runner. Favored pieces, particularly story cloths, are hung on walls, exciting the interest of children too young to remember life in Laos. Some pieces are added to the elders' collection of funeral pillows while others are incorporated into gift exchanges with American friends. Still, many women state ruefully that they cannot afford to keep the beautiful cloths; their importance as potential income is simply too great.

Left:
In the United States, Hmong women don traditional dress in celebration of the Hmong New Year. It is a time when Hmong gather from all over the country to strengthen friendships and reaffirm their cultural identity. Philadelphia, 1987.

Below:
The skirt of the Green Hmong is ornamented with an intricate pattern of appliqué which is folded accordion-style and layered with aprons, silver bags, and belts of coins. Philadelphia, 1986.

American Hmong no longer wear traditional clothing on a daily basis, but paj ntaub retains its most potent meaning as a dramatic focus of attention during the year's most anticipated event—the New Year. Many people, particularly young women, take care to dress traditionally for the ever-popular celebration, and women still sew the finely wrought pieces that grace the New Year outfits. If a woman has little time to spare, she may purchase hats, sashes, purses, jackets and skirts from craftswomen in the U.S. or in Thai refugee camps who have developed a trade in traditional garments. Though each article of clothing has antecedents in traditional culture, Hmong festive dress is not a static tradition. Young women express their fashion consciousness with constantly changing styles. These transformations are often direct responses to the expansion of decorative resources available in Thai and American markets, the increased use of sewing machines, and the contraction of available time for sewing outfits.[7] The "New Style" includes such recent innovations as the use of French velvet embossed with metallic thread and glitter, and tall rooster-shaped hats trimmed elaborately with spangles and sequins. Many young women brighten the look of the Green Hmong batiked skirt by ornamenting the waxed patterns from waist to hem with appliqued strips and cross-stitch embroidery in acid green, hot pink, and bright oranges, yellows, and reds (the earlier style sported only red and pink appliqué and cross-stitch bordering the hem). Current trends stress the light-catching, sound-making properties of glass and plastic beads, bells, and the old silver coins of Indochina. Innovation and retention respond to a traditional aesthetic which highlights the interplay between dark and light, sound and silence, old and new, fiber and metal.

Above:
Chia Ker Lor's basketmaking tools, Philadelphia, 1986.

Left:
With ingenuity and innovation, Chia Ker Lor uses discarded plastic strapping to make baskets, which were formerly made of bamboo native to Laos. Philadelphia, 1986.

Developments in Hmong basketry traditions differ significantly from those marking contemporary paj ntaub. As did marketed paj ntaub, plastic basket production began in the refugee camps of Thailand, where bundles of recycled plastic strips are sold in local markets. Though many craftspeople continued weaving bamboo baskets, camp regulations restricted easy access to this usually abundant resource. Unlike paj ntaub, neither bamboo nor plastic baskets were exported from the camps by middlemen; trade was limited to direct, personal interaction.

The wide availability of inexpensive containers and the dearth of suitable bamboo have largely squelched the basketmaking craft. Lightweight baskets now made with plastic strapping, however, are still valued as useful household implements, particularly for transporting belongings and storage. Some artists have experimented with reproducing such traditional artifacts as rice cookers, winnowers, and even arrow sheaths. Though their baskets are popular within their own communities, the Hmong rarely seek an external market for them.

Since their arrival in the United States, the primary concern of most Hmong has been to achieve economic security for their families. Learning to speak a new language, cope with unfamiliar technologies, and develop new occupational skills requires intense dedication and personal resourcefulness. Young students, faced with the demands of school and part-time work (often taken to relieve their family's economic burden), find little time to practice the painstaking art of paj ntaub and little need to make baskets. Yet despite these odds, the

Left:
At the New Year celebration in Philadelphia, young men and women play a traditional courtship game which introduces people to each other. It involves standing in lines opposite each other and tossing a ball back and forth. Philadelphia, 1986.

Hmong consciously strive to preserve their culture. Elders and youth alike debate issues concerning what it means to be Hmong. New Year celebrations and family gatherings are photographed and videotaped intensively. Tapes and photographs circulate from city to city, providing more communication between geographically distant communities than was possible ever before. Partnerships with American scholars have begun to produce archival materials that record tradition, knowledge, history and philosophy. The Philadelphia community has received grants through the Pennsylvania Heritage Affairs Commission to establish apprenticeships enabling master craftswomen to instruct young girls in the art of paj ntaub (see Color Plate #16).

Above:
Young apprentice needle-
workers receive their les-
sons amid shelves and
piles of *paj ntaub* squares
ready for sale to the American market. Philadelphia,
1984.

Documenting traditions that now live mostly in memory is an important task. With such information the Hmong can use meaningful ideas from the past as a resource for today's choices. Upon reexamination, moribund traditions come to shed light upon history, proving their value as heritage; they may even become candidates for revitalization. But documenting the past is not enough. As their lives change, people develop ways to cope with new situations. Even ephemeral activities, developed as temporary responses to current events and social situations, are important to record. Today's innovation may become tomorrow's tradition.

The most dynamic forces influencing Hmong tradition are the people themselves. The ways in which individuals invite, accept, or resist change reveals one of the fundamental dramas of human life. What modifications of traditional aesthetic principles will occur as people continue to shape the Hmong-American experience? That answer lies with future generations, but this age owes them the opportunity of forging their present with a full knowledge of the past.

Right:
Master *paj ntaub* needle-workers (left to right) Pang Xiong Sirirathasuk, Mao Vang Xiong and Yee Vang Lo proudly show the work of their apprentices completed as part of the Apprenticeships in Traditional Arts, a joint program of the Pennsylvania Heritage Affairs Commission and the Pennsylvania Council on the Arts. Philadelphia, 1987.

Notes

1. Jacques Lemoine, *Un Village Hmong Vert du haut Laos* (Paris: Centre national de la Recherche Scientifique, 1972).

2. See, for example, the interview with Xia Kao Xiong, Philadelphia, Pa., October 6, 1985 (Hmong Community Folklife Documentation Project, HCFDP85-BL&ML001, Folklife Center, International House, Philadelphia, Pa.); and Yih-Fu Ruey, *The Miao: Their Origin and Southern Migration*, Second Biennial Conference Proceedings (Taipei: International Association of Historians of Asia, 1962).

3. For a personal account of one woman's flight from Laos, see May Xiong and Nancy D. Donnelly, "My Life in Laos," in *The Hmong World*, Vol. 1, eds. Brenda Johns and David Strecker (New Haven: Council on Southeast Asia Studies at Yale University, 1986), pp. 201-43.

4. Eric Crystal, "Buffalo Heads and Sacred Threads: Hmong Culture of the Southeast Asian Highlands," in *Textiles as Texts: Arts of Hmong Women from Laos*, ed. Amy Catlin (Los Angeles: The Woman's Building, 1987). Crystal cites an official estimate of 62,000 Hmong currently residing in the United States.

5. Timothy Dunnigan, "Antecedents of Hmong Resetttlement in the United States," in *Hmong Art: Tradition and Change*, ed. Joanne Cubbs (Sheboygan, Wis.: John Michael Kohler Arts Center, 1986) pp.5-9.

6. Jean Mottin, *Allons faire le tour du ciel et de la terre: Le Chamanisme des Hmong vu dans les textes* (Bangkok: White Lotus Co., Ltd., 1982).

7. Joanne Cubbs also describes these phenomena in her essay "Hmong Art: Tradition and Change," in *Hmong Art: Tradition and Change*, pp. 21-29.

Suggested Reading

Catlin, Amy, ed. *Textiles as Texts: Arts of Hmong Women from Laos.* Los Angeles: The Woman's Building, 1987.

Cubbs, Joanne, ed. *Hmong Art: Tradition and Change.* Sheboygan, Wis.: John Michael Kohler Arts Center, 1986.

Cultural Palace of Nationalities. *Clothings and Ornaments of China's Miao People.* Beijing: Nationality Press, 1985.

Downing, Bruce T. and Douglas P. Olney, eds. *The Hmong in the West.* Minneapolis: Southeast Asian Refugee Studies Project, Center for Urban and Regional Affairs, University of Minnesota, 1982.

Hendricks, Glenn L., Bruce T. Downing and Amos S. Deinard. *The Hmong in Transition.* New York: Center for Migration Studies of New York, Inc. and the Southeast Asian Refugee Studies Project of the University of Minnesota, 1986.

Johns, Brenda, and David Strecker. *The Hmong World.* New Haven: Council on Southeast Asia Studies at Yale University, 1986.

Peterson, Sally. "Translating Experience and the Reading of a Story Cloth." *Journal of American Folklore* 101(1988):6-22.

_______. "A Cool Heart and a Watchful Mind: Creating Hmong *Paj Ntaub* in the Context of Community." In *Pieced by Mother: Symposium Papers*, edited by Jeannette Lasansky, pp. 34-45. Lewisburg, Pa.: Oral Traditions Project of the Union County Historical Society, 1988.

Thomas E. Graves

Pennsylvania German crafts and craftsworkers appear with great frequency on today's craft scene: at the festivals and the craft shows, as well as in the national mail order craft catalogs, the "country look" magazines, the directories detailing where to find the "best" in contemporary crafts, and in the gift shops selling silk screened hex signs, trays and trivets, scarves and napkins, and other tourist objects with Pennsylvania German themes.

There is no doubt about it; Pennsylvania German folk art, whether real, recreated, "in-the-style-of," or imitation, is big business for promoters and craftspeople alike. If it were not for the contemporary interest in "rustic" and country look design and if it were not for the tourist market, it is almost certain that many of the craftspeople would not be in business today and that some of the genres, such as hex signs and fraktur, would have died out. Many people believe that interest in things Pennsylvania German dates from the 1960s, a time when handmade objects and rural life came into fashion; however, interest in Pennsylvania German crafts really dates much earlier.

In the decades between the American Centennial celebration in 1876 and the turn of the century, the Colonial Revival with its attendant craze for antiques focused public attention on colonial Pennsylvania German art. In the 1920s tourism became big business, as cars and the improved roads enabled people to go for Sunday drives to the country. The travel section in the Sunday newspaper, which developed in this era, sent people roaming through various parts of the state.

Below:
Hex signs by Bill Schuster.
Left: "Two Birds" (checklist
#175). Right: "Wilkum"
(checklist #176)

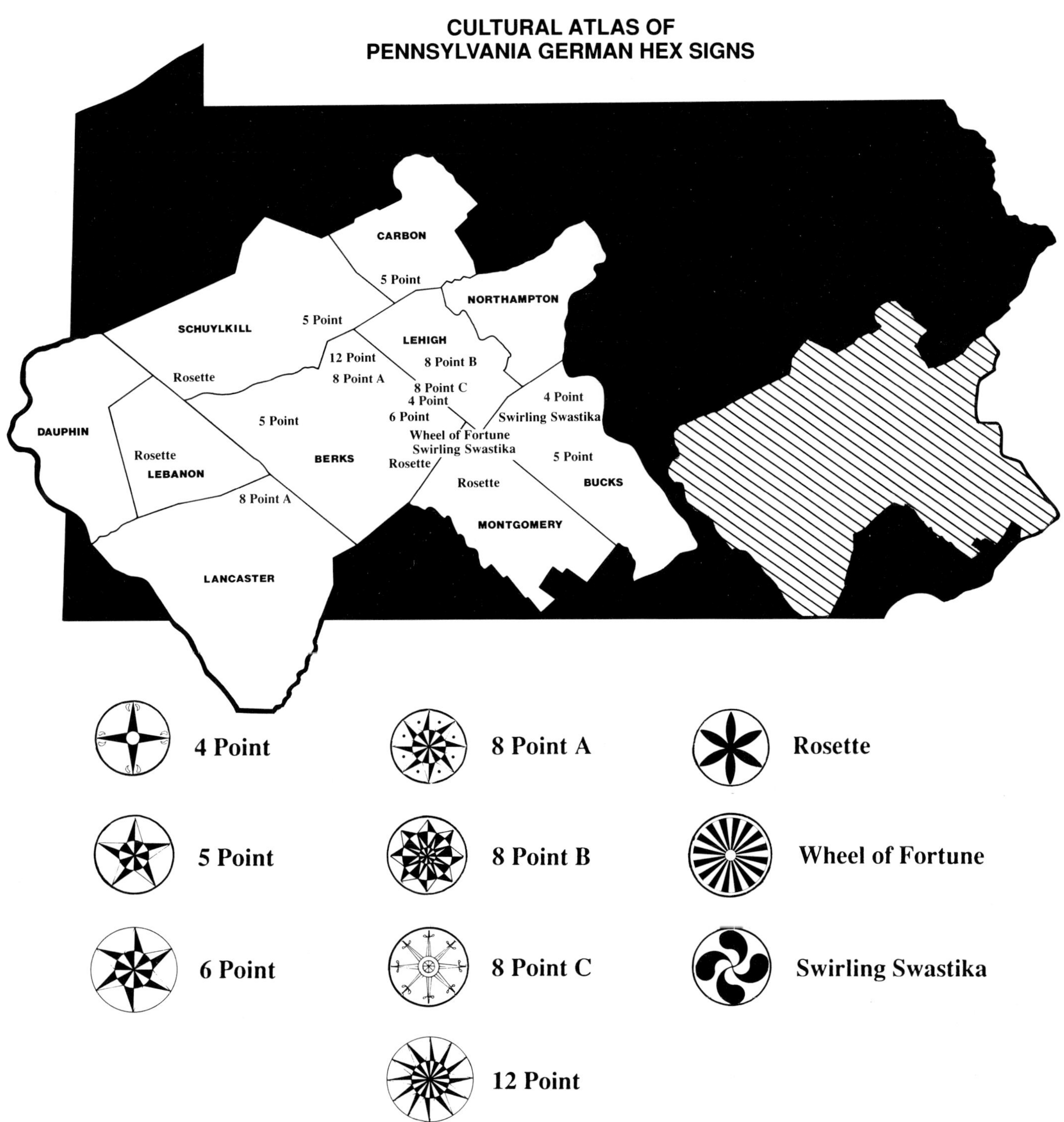

CULTURAL ATLAS OF
PENNSYLVANIA GERMAN HEX SIGNS
CARBON
5 Point
NORTHAMPTON
SCHUYLKILL
5 Point
LEHIGH
12 Point
8 Point B
Rosette
8 Point A
8 Point C
4 Point
4 Point
5 Point
6 Point
Swirling Swastika
DAUPHIN
Wheel of Fortune
Swirling Swastika
Rosette
LEBANON
BERKS
Rosette
5 Point
Rosette
8 Point A
Rosette
BUCKS
MONTGOMERY
LANCASTER
4 Point
8 Point A
Rosette
5 Point
8 Point B
Wheel of Fortune
6 Point
8 Point C
Swirling Swastika
12 Point

The landscape is inherently conservative. Except where urban sprawl has encroached on the rural farmlands, a drive through Berks or Lehigh County today will contain many of the same sights that would have been seen in the 1920s by those early "Sunday drivers" or even by wagoners of the previous century. These sights include the quaint "German Georgian" farmhouses, the immense forebay barns, and on many of the barns curious geometric patterns which were originally called *bluma* (flowers), or *sterne* (stars). They became known as *hexafoos* in the 1920s and since the 1950s have been called hex signs. Hex signs are found on the barns of the "church" groups, most notably Reformed (now a part of the United Church of Christ) and Lutheran, in Berks, Lehigh, Schuylkill, and surrounding counties. The "plain" groups (the Amish and the Mennonites) of Lancaster and its surrounding counties do not have hex signs on their barns, contrary to the paintings of Charles Wysocki and decades of tourist and popular literature.[1]

Instead of the dozen men painting hex signs at any one time during the first half of this century, there are now only three well known painters: Johnny Claypoole of Lenhartsville, Berks County, Bill Schuster of Emmaus, Lehigh County, and Ivan Hoyt of Wapwallopen, Luzerne County. For the most part, however, these three men do not paint barns for farmers and rural families. They paint on discs of masonite and plywood for the crowd of tourists and visitors to the festivals and craft shows at which they sell their wares. Another difference, besides the different medium and audience, is the set of designs used by these men. In place of the symmetrical and geometric designs employed on barns, a full spectrum of non-geometric designs appears, including birds, trees-of-life, shamrocks, hearts, and, in the case of Ivan Hoyt, pigs, chickens, cats, and angels. All three continue to make and sell geometric stars in small numbers, but these are usually passed over in favor of the more colorful non-geometric designs, though Bill Schuster notes that recently more people have been requesting the stars. Hex signs painted by these men literally have gone around the world. International tourists buy their work at craft shows and occasionally seek them out at their workshops.

How did the hex sign get down off the barn into the craft show and how did it lose its geometric look? The answers take us back to the first half of the century. The interest shown by collectors and museums in Pennsylvania German antiques caused a stir among the Pennsylvania Germans themselves. This interest was reinforced by the various Pennsylvania German ethnic societies and publications that started appearing towards the end of the nineteenth century. Soon the rising tourist industry needed items to sell to the visitors passing through the region. These two interconnected developments emerged, shaping both what Pennsylvania German craftspeople create and what is sold as souvenirs.

The revival of Pennsylvania German art and culture began in the 1930s. I use "revival" to mean a process in which Pennsylvania German craftspeople and their Pennsylvania German customers consciously reach back to their historical tradition to draw on those artistic and cultural forms which they see as having relevance in today's world. They are rejuvenating forms which were getting "tired," such as hex signs and fraktur, and they are reviving, bringing back to life, "dead" forms such as decorated chests. Rather than borrowing forms from another culture, they are drawing on their own cultural past to help give meaning to contemporary existence. They, craftsperson and customer alike, are recreating, and contributing to the evolution of their group's cultural forms. The revivalists, though they do not call themselves such, are not a re-enactment group; they are part of a continuing cultural evolution. Products of the revival include the creations of Yorkcraft and Paul Weiend and the writings of people such as Ann Hark and Cornelius Weygandt. Later this revival spawned the Pennsylvania Folklife Society, its journal, *Pennsylvania Folklife*, and the Kutztown Folk Festival.

When people think of Pennsylvania German art, they generally think of what has become known as the "classic period" which lasted from about 1740 to 1840. This period saw the production of most of the decorated chests, hand-done fraktur, hand-carved gravestones, punched tin, and other genres. After 1840, many of these classic genres were no longer produced. The decorated chests gave way first to simple wood-grained chests and then to chests of drawers. The production of hand-done fraktur, while never dying out, became scarce in comparison to printed certificates. Punched tin gave way to painted tin.

Meanwhile, other sets of designs and genres arose. During the second quarter of the nineteenth century, Pennsylvania Germans added two genres to the ranks of their popular art forms: quilts and hex signs. The quilts were adopted from the Pennsylvania German's English neighbors. The hex sign came from within their own culture as part of an earlier Pennsylvania German revival which also had included a return to Pennsylvania German designs on gravestones. Concurrently the Amish and Mennonites adopted and rigidified the contemporary fashion as a uniform.

This earlier revival involved a conscious looking back at tradition and the selective use of these earlier forms to respond to the needs of the time. In their need to make public statements concerning their ethnicity in the face of local anti-German and anti-foreign sentiments of the "Know- Nothing" era, the church Pennsylvania Germans chose design elements from their past—geometric designs and trees-of-life, and applied them in new situations, to the barn and the gravestone. The plain people, meanwhile, rigidified the absence of such design elements in their creative expressions.

By the end of the nineteenth century few Pennsylvania Germans cared much for their group's own art work, but this attitude changed with the revival that started in the 1930s and continues today. Earlier designs were adapted and used on new furniture and clothing, in prints and paintings, and on other objects. Genres which had faded out of practice, such as fraktur, found a new lease on life. The hex signs, one genre which had not yet shown signs of weakening, continued to be popular through the revival. But unlike the nineteenth century revival, this one did not remain as free from outside influences. In particular, the twentieth century revival had to come to grips with the tourist industry and its call for souvenirs. Many souvenir items were designed and produced by Pennsylvania German artists and craftspeople who were playing to two markets, the "in-group" and the "out-group."

Many of the revival craftspeople were self-taught. They were not necessarily practicing traditions of their parents or others within their community. They were seeking out their ancestral roots rather than their parental ones to gain ideas and designs.

Like the people who adapted the earlier motifs to barns and gravestones in the nineteenth century, these twentieth century revival artists did not merely copy the past or resurrect old forms. Instead they adapted, taking from both colonial Pennsylvania German and Victorian motifs those that seemed appropriate. A new set of common designs was created, a set shared by both the craftspeople and the souvenir makers. For example, the "distelfink" on a tree-of-life appeared in colonial fraktur and pottery in various forms, but only since the 1940s has it appeared in a highly stylized form on hex signs and fraktur.

Some of the early producers of souvenirs had a significant impact on the creation of the new designs and forms. Two of the most influential were Jacob Zook of Paradise, Lancaster County, and Johnny Ott of Lenhartsville, Berks County (d. 1964). Between them, they made hex signs the Pennsylvania German souvenir par excellence, but their hex signs were a new entity. They took the round format and a few of the geometrical designs from the barns and added many non-geometric designs. Expanding on ideas first widely presented by Wallace Nutting in his book *Pennsylvania Beautiful*, they created meanings for all their new signs.[2] There was now a star with raindrops for "rain and fertility," a sign with hearts for "love and marriage," and an "Irish" hex sign for "good luck." Johnny Ott became immensely successful through his work at the Kutztown Folk Festival, eclipsing the traditional sign painter Milton Hill who stayed with the more traditional designs he had used on barns. Jacob Zook achieved success making silk screened hex signs and selling them retail and wholesale to an international market. Their designs became what people expected in hex signs. Although some of Ott's extreme designs are no longer reproduced, the work of Claypoole, Schuster and Hoyt is highly influenced by his. These three contemporary painters do not make copies of Ott's work. They have all developed highly individualized styles; nevertheless, their primary audience remains the same as Ott's: the festival and craft show crowd.

What happened to "real" hex signs during this time? They still were created but not with the same fanfare as the craft show signs. As recently as the late 1950s, almost a dozen traditional painters made hex signs. Some, including Milton Hill and Harry Adam, turned to discs in their later years, but these painters did not abandon the traditional forms. By the early 1980s, however, very few new hex signs were being painted on barns, although some old ones were being kept in good repair. Two of the contemporary painters have helped to change this situation.

Johnny Claypoole loves to go up on barns and paint or repaint hex signs (see Color Plate #2). When he repaints a sign, he tries to use the design and colors that were there originally. When he paints a new sign, he uses either a sixteen point star or a black rosette with red hearts, designs that are his signature. Pass by a barn with these designs and you have passed by a Claypoole painted barn. Claypoole probably paints more new signs on barns than any other single painter. He was taught by Johnny Ott and influenced by Milton Hill, learning to paint for both the traditional market and the new tourist market. He produces a different product for each one: geometric signs for the traditional and non-geometric ones for the tourist. Having started in the tourist/craft show business, Claypoole has had an increasing amount of work in the traditional barn painting business. Farmers are rejuvenating the field of decorating barns, and Claypoole is filling their need from the traditional set of barn designs as he has adapted them to his own tastes.

Both Claypoole and Schuster also have made several sets of discs to be placed on barns. Even on these barn discs, the designs remain geometric. These discs are a way for the farmer to save money. Instead of paying the painter to put up scaffolding and paint directly on the barn, these large discs can be placed directly over earlier, worn stars. All three hex sign painters say that they have to produce what the

Above:
Hex signs by John Clay-poole. Left to right: "Wil-kom" (checklist #183); "Sun and Rain" (checklist #182); "Tree-of-Life" (checklist #181)

customers request and that they often get good ideas from those requests.

Fraktur is another genre which is part of the current revival. Most eighteenth-century fraktur was completely hand-done and included birth and baptismal certificates, rewards for merit, book plates, religious sentiments, and other forms. In the nineteenth century pre-printed certificates became more common than the hand-made ones and filled the same purposes, but today the hand-made forms again dominate. Since the time of the earliest presses among the Pennsylvania-Germans, both the hand-made and the pre-printed forms have co-existed with now one, now the other dominating. Although the major documenting and religious functions of fraktur have remained constant, the designs have steadily evolved. The early certificates drew upon the common fund of folk art motifs. After 1800 Victorian fashion dominated. Since 1940 the folk art motifs again have been the favored designs. Although contemporary fraktur artists, such as Ruthanne Hartung of Reading, Berks County, have utilized the folk art motifs, they

Above:
Pennsylvania German *fraktur* (birth certificate), 1794 (checklist #187)

Right:
Pennsylvania German
fraktur (birth certificate) by
Ruthanne Hartung, 1987
(checklist #189)

have not merely copied. They have adapted the designs and forms to meet their own preferences and those of their customers.

Hartung gets much of her work not only from her appearances in festivals and craft shows but also from her listing in national mail order craft catalogs and from word-of-mouth advertising. As are the makers of hex signs, she is selling to two markets, a traditional market which still wants to record births, marriages, and family trees, and a newer tourist and country look market which may want to start such recording or may want to buy fraktur for its decorative value. However, there are not two sets of fashionable fraktur, as there are two kinds of hex signs, one for each audience. Maybe this homogeneity exists because there was not a Johnny Ott of fraktur who used the genre to make a showcase for himself.

The current revival of Pennsylvania German crafts and folk art is caught between two worlds. While the culture is being made anew for the Pennsylvania Germans, it is also being recreated and interpreted for those outside the culture. This recreation and interpretation takes place at festivals and craft shows where Johnny Claypoole, Bill Schuster, and Ivan Hoyt paint their hex signs before an audience and discuss each sign's "meaning." It likewise takes place when Ruthanne Hartung explains the early forms of fraktur and their documentary uses and how she has adapted form and function. These craftsworkers sell not only the craft itself, but the culture as well, or an image of the culture acceptable to the audience.

Notes

1. Charles Wysocki, *An American Celebration: The Art of Charles Wysocki* (New York: Greenwich Press, 1985).

2. See, for example, Wallace Nutting, *Pennsylvania Beautiful (Eastern)* (Framingham, Mass.: Old America Company, 1924), pp. 28-29.

Suggested Reading

Claypoole, Johnny. *Johnny Claypoole, "Hexologist."* Lenhartsville, Pa.: by the author, 1979.

Graburn, Nelson H.H., ed. *Ethnic and Tourist Arts: Cultural Expressions from the Fourth World.* Berkeley, University of California Press, 1976.

Graves, Thomas E. "Ethnic Artists, Artifacts, and Authenticity: Pennsylvania German and Ukrainian Folk Craft Today." *Pioneer America* 15, no. 1 (1983):21-34.

__________. "The Pennsylvania-German Hex Sign: A Study in Folk Process." Ph.D. diss., University of Pennsylvania, 1984.

Shelly, Donald A. *The Fraktur-Writings or Illuminated Manuscripts of the Pennsylvania Germans.* Allentown: Schlechters, 1961.

Smith, Elmer L. and Mel Horst. *Hex Signs and Other Barn Decorations.* Lebanon, Pa.: Applied Arts, 1965.

Smith, Valene L., ed. *Hosts and Guests: The Anthropology of Tourism.* Philadelphia, University of Pennsylvania Press, 1977.

Stoudt, John Joseph. *Pennsylvania German Folk Art.* Allentown: Schlechters, 1966.

Yoder, Don and Thomas E. Graves. *Hex Signs.* New York, E.P. Dutton, 1988.

REDWARE REVIVAL AND RE-PRESENTATION:
A Pennsylvania Pottery Tradition

Susan L. F. Isaacs

Redware, a low-fired earthenware pottery bearing a deep reddish brown hue with yellow, green, black, and sometimes blue decoration, is enjoying widespread popularity in the U.S. About a dozen potteries around the country (mostly in Pennsylvania and other points east) produce redware in one form or another, and it is one of the most popular craft commodities today. What accounts for its appeal and who are the people making and buying it?

English redwares came to New England, Virginia, and the Chesapeake with the first colonists. Earthenware production subsequently evolved in these regions; however, it was the first German-speaking immigrants to Pennsylvania, first arriving in 1683, who developed the most elaborate red earthenwares. Over the next two centuries, American redware grew from these beginnings into a rich tradition in its own right. Widely collected, actively reproduced, documented in *The Index of American Design*, and treasured in museum collections, redware decorated with thin clay "slip" became recognized as a "classic" American "folk art" genre.[1]

Broadly speaking, there were three traditional types of redware: undecorated utilitarian, *slip-trailed*, and *sgraffito* wares. From settlement through the mid-nineteenth century plain redwares were used for every imaginable purpose in the home, on the farm, in the kitchen, and in the barn. Baking dishes, churns, storage crocks, pie plates, milk pans, door knobs, ink wells, roach traps, and chamber pots were but a few examples.

Slip-trailed redware was made throughout the colonies. The name refers to the thin clay slip drizzled through a quill to create lettering or abstract designs. It is nearly impossible to distinguish simple slip-trailed Pennsylvania wares from their mid-Atlantic or New England counterparts although a few potteries are recognized for specific styles.[2] Sgraffito was produced by brushing the surface of a damp clay object with white or yellow liquid slip. Then a stylus was used to carve designs. In the U.S., the majority of elaborately decorated slip-trailed or sgraffito plates are Pennsylvanian. They were used for gifts and to commemorate rituals such as births, baptisms, and weddings.

By the mid-nineteenth century more advanced technologies were already displacing redwares with sturdier stoneware (which also had the advantage of a lead-free, non-toxic glaze), cleaner glass, and tougher tin. Imports and domestically produced china also became widely available to consumers. At one time, hundreds of local redware potteries dotted central and southeastern Pennsylvania. Now, although only a few potteries remain, contemporary potter Lester Breininger believes there is a weak but continuous chain of tradition to today's redware producers.

Above:
Redware dish attributed to
John Leidy, Sr. (checklist
#185)

Contemporary potters make a wide range of objects, from close replicas that copy or extrapolate from wares seen in museum collections or books to personal interpretations of "traditional" wares. It is imprecise to say potters are actually *reviving* the past, for the past has not died.[3] It may be more useful to think of redware potters as *re-presenting* the past; their work results from a kind of dialectic between past and present. Re-presentation suggests that while contemporary redware offers the appearance of the old redware on which it is based, the rationale for producing these objects is radically different from what it was prior to the industrial revolution. It reflects the emotional and aesthetic needs of consumers in post-industrial society rather than utilitarian demands.

Consumers today want to buy both pottery and the *experience* of history.[4] Potters must therefore reflect some level of intimacy with tradition, which their customers interpret as a hallmark of authenticity. Potters who are Pennsylvania German easily identify themselves genealogically, historically, or aesthetically with ethnic and ceramic traditions. Potters who are not Pennsylvania German expend more energy in establishing ties to tradition and a sense of continuity with the living history image that they all project. Creating this image is inextricably bound up with marketing a cultural artifact, a "commodification" of culture.

The Turtlecreek Pottery in Ohio is part of David T. Smith and Company, a small business concerned primarily with making and marketing both reproduction furniture and pottery. Its potters are devoted to making both redware and other reproduction earthenwares. When Turtlecreek opened in 1984 it offered a "regular line" and a "museum line" of wares, the latter chemically aged and chipped "for collectors who want the look and feel of authenticity."[5] When the regular line was discontinued in 1988 in favor of the more expensive museum line, it was a sign that Turtlecreek had created a niche for its wares among consumers. In less than five years, the Turtlecreek Pottery successfully manipulated a repertoire of artistically and historically based images to cultivate a unique market. Its considerable economic success was due to the quality of the wares, the skill of the potters, and the fact that owner David T. Smith relishes business per se as much as he does handmade objects.

In a survey of two hundred customers attending redware sales at three redware potteries in Pennsylvania, I learned that roughly half of those attending identified themselves as Pennsylvania German. Ninety percent of the consumers collected both contemporary hand-

128

Right:
Redware artist Lester Breininger annually hosts his "porch show" which attracts visitors from throughout the mid-Atlantic states in search of Pennsylvania folk art. Robesonia, 1985.

Below:
Redware dish by Lester Breininger (checklist #186)

made objects and antiques. They used redware primarily for serving food or for decoration. Only in the homes of potters and a few very wealthy families have I seen redware in daily use as tableware.

The division of redware consumers among Pennsylvania Germans and non-Pennsylvania Germans suggests that the pottery has equal cachet in and outside its own culture. It is both an emblem of ethnicity and a symbol of history. Redware potters, particularly Lester Breininger, act as popular ethnographers interpreting the meaning of redware and its context to consumers. When customers visit the Breininger Pottery, they witness demonstrations of redware production by Breininger or one of his helpers. Breininger is fiercely proud of his heritage as a ninth generation Pennsylvania Dutchman, and regales visitors with anecdotes about his culture or the excitement of his most recent pottery acquisition— perhaps a tool or a finished object. His own history, the quiet rural setting of his Victorian home in Berks County, and his fervor for using old tools to produce new wares lend authenticity to the consumer's touristic experience at the pottery. It is an experience that stands in stark contrast to the more widely available entry points into Pennsylvania German culture: plastic motel signs with Amish profiles, the Dutch Wonderland amusement park, and other tourist sites. A great deal of purported information about Pennsylvania Germans is produced by outsiders for outsiders. In contrast, Breininger offers an apparently "authentic" experience to all who find their way to his work place. Lester Breininger does in a sense commodify culture, but that is not the purpose of his work as a potter.

Consumers are not just buyers of pottery. They do receive the tangible benefits of a redware object, but they also reap intangible benefits when they visit potteries in person. A trip to a potter in the country exposes consumers to living history where a remote period in America's past seems available for direct experience. When seeing a pottery they become willing participants in the *image* of colonial economy.[6] Potters such as Breininger act as educators or popular ethnographers in demonstrating redware production and describing its development over hundreds of years. They are self-appointed culture brokers, communicating to consumers about craft, art, and history. Potters construct and interpret their own small-scale living history sites. When buyers take home a piece of redware, it reflects the idea of colonial domesticity, warming even a high-tech setting with the idea of history and hand production.

Notes

1. Erwin O. Christensen, *The Index of American Design* (New York: MacMillan, 1950).

2. Ellen Paul Denker, "Ceramics at the Crossroads: American Pottery at New York's Gateway, 1750-1900," *Staten Island Historian* 3 (1986):21-36.

3. Mark Slobin, "Rethinking 'Revival' of American Ethnic Music," *New York Folklore Quarterly* 9(1983):37-44.

4. Dean MacCannell, *The Tourist: A New Theory of the Leisure Class* (New York: Schocken Books, 1976).

5. Turtlecreek Potters/David T. Smith and Company, Catalog (Morrow, Oh., [1985]).

6. John Darwin Dorst, "Myths of Tradition and Modes of Exchange in Chadds Ford, Pennsylvania" (Ph.D. diss., University of Pennsylvania, 1983).

Suggested Reading

Briggs, Charles L. *The Wood Carvers of Cordova, New Mexico: Social Dimensions of an Artistic "Revival."* Knoxville, Tn.: University of Tennessee Press, 1980.

Garvan, Beatrice R. *The Pennsylvania German Collection.* Philadelphia: Philadelphia Museum of Art, 1982.

Isaacs. Susan L. F. "Retrospective Tradition: Potters and Buyers in the Contemporary Redware Marketplace." *New Jersey Folklife* 11(1986):21-34.

Kirshenblatt-Gimblett, Barbara. "Tourism in New York City: Introduction." *Journal of American Culture* 10(Summer 1987):67-68.

Moeran, Brian. *Lost Innocence: Folk Craft Potters of Onta, Japan.* Berkeley: University of California Press, 1984.

Swank, Scott T., et. al. *Arts of the Pennsylvania Germans.* New York: W.W. Norton, 1983.

Checklist of Objects in the Exhibition

Note: The following format is used for each entry:

Object name, maker, location, date
Cultural tradition
Material(s). Measurements
(length x width x height)
Source (lender or owner)

Introduction

1. **Pennsylvania longrifle** by Joseph J. Zebrowski, Jersey Shore, 1986
Wood, iron, brass, silver and antler. 58 1/2" x 7 1/2"
Joseph J. Zebrowski

2. **Walking stick** by Isaac Maefield, Philadelphia, 1983
Afro-American
Wood, brass. 2" x 36"
Isaac Maefield

3. *Nebo Lutheran Church* by Becky S. Vasgaard, Mt. Jewett (Boone, North Carolina), 1988
Swedish
Papercut. 11" x 13"
Becky S. Vasgaard

4. **Carved chain** by Robert A. Demarest, Tannersville, 1980
Walnut and white pine, 32" x 1" x 1"
Robert A. Demarest

5. **"Ball in cage"** by Robert A. Demarest, Tannersville, 1980
Walnut and white pine. 8" x 2" x 2"
Robert A. Demarest

6. **Cant hook (logroller)** by Michael Stephano, Starrucca, 1988
Lumbering
Wood and metal. 39 1/2" x 7" x 2"
Michael Stephano

7. *Ketubah* **(marriage contract)** by Susan Leviton, 1988
Jewish
Ink, gouache, artist's pigment, gold/silver foil on paper.
25" x 21"
Susan Leviton

8. **Icon of St. John the Theologian,** by a sister of the Orthodox Monastery of the Holy Transfiguration, Ellwood City, 1988
Romanian
Egg tempera and gold leaf on wood. 4" x 7" x 1 1/2"
Orthodox Monastery of the Holy Transfiguration

9. **Carpet** by a sister of the Orthodox Monastery of the Holy Transfiguration, Ellwood City, 1976
Romanian
Woven wool. 37" x 18 1/2" x 1/8"
Orthodox Monastery of the Holy Transfiguration

10. **Christening ensemble** by Judith Brandau, Butler, 1986
English smocking, Irish lace, French handsewing
Cotton with embroidery
Bonnet: 6 1/2" x 19" (with ribbon)
Gown: 26" x 21 1/2"
Judith and Danielle Brandau

11. **"Fire engine" funeral sculpture (for displaying flowers)** by Joseph Janco, Sr., c.1920 (replacement hose made by Joseph Janco, Jr., 1988)
Slovak
Wire. 56" x 23" x 21"
Balch Institute for Ethnic Studies

12. **Mask** by Osvaldo Ayala, Lancaster, 1987
Puerto Rican
Coconut. 6 1/2" x 9 1/2" x 5 1/2"
Spanish-American Civic Association

13. **Basket** by Lewis Reinhart, New Oxford, 1988
German Gypsy
Willow. 12" (diameter) x 17" (with handle)
Lewis Reinhart

14. *Valley Belle* **of Pittsburgh (tow boat)** by Ernest S. Gabler, Greensboro, 1978
River life
Carved wood, wire, plastic, metal, pebbles and glue.
28" x 11" x 6 1/2"
Ernest S. Gabler

15. **Christmas ornaments** by Annie Morgalis, Minersville, 1988
Lithuanian
Straw
Two wreaths with 6 hexagon pendants: 7" x 11" x 3/4"
Octagon with 4 box pendants: 10 1/2" x 15" x 3"
Wolf: 5" x 5 1/2"
Sixteen-pointed star:
4 1/2" (diameter)
Lantern: 5 1/2" x 2 1/2" x 2 1/2"
Balch Institute for Ethnic Studies

16. **Carving of a mine shaft entrance** by Harry Thompson, Minersville, 1988
Welsh
Wood and anthracite coal.
3 1/2" x 1 1/4" x 7/8"
Harry Thompson

17. **Liturgical palls (chalice covers)** by the Felician Sisters of the Holy Trinity Church, Erie
Polish
Painted (1978): 6 3/4" x 6 3/4"
Embroidered (silk thread on linen, 1952): 7 1/4" x 7 1/4"
Monsignor John Daniszewski, Holy Trinity Church

Generations

18. **Sample stone showing lettering styles** by Harvard Wood, Jr., Lansdowne, 1938
"Salt and pepper" granite.
20″ x 38 1/2″ x 1 1/2″
Harvard C. Wood, III

19. **Sample flower carving** by Harvard C. Wood, Jr., Lansdowne, 1957
Granite. 7 1/4″ x 7 1/4″ x 1 1/2″
Harvard C. Wood, III

20. **Sample carving of praying hands** by Harvard C. Wood, III, Lansdowne, 1970
Granite 4 1/4″ x 9″ x 2 3/4″
Harvard C. Wood, III

21. **Carved lamb ornaments** by Thomas Wood, Lansdowne, 1880
Marble. 4 1/2″ x 2″ x 1 1/2″;
7″ x 2 1/4″ x 2 1/4″
Harvard C. Wood, III

22. **Sketch of funeral memorial** by Harvard C. Wood, Jr., Lansdowne, c. 1945
Ink on paper. 16 3/4″ x 15 3/4″
Harvard C. Wood, III

23. **Sketch of funeral memorial** by Harvard C. Wood, III, Lansdowne, 1988
Pencil on paper. 15 1/4″ x 14″
Harvard C. Wood, III

24. **Art Memorials** by Harvard C. Wood, Jr., Lansdowne, c. 1923
Pamphlet with photographs.
4″ x 9″
Harvard C. Wood, III

25. **H. C. Wood Inc. Memorials** by Harvard C. Wood, III, Lansdowne, 1988
Pamphlet with photographs.
8 1/2″ x 11″
Harvard C. Wood, III

26. **Pulley with hook,** 1820
Wood and metal. 5″ x 12″ x 4″
Harvard C. Wood, III

27. **Bush hammer,** 1840
Wood and metal. 7 1/2″ x 16″ x 2 1/2″
Harvard C. Wood, III

28. **Mallet,** 1860
Wood. 4″ x 9 3/4″
Harvard C. Wood, III

29. **Hand drill with leather strap,** 1860
Wood and metal.
20 1/2″ x 24 1/2″ x 4 1/2″
Harvard C. Wood, III

30. **Bush chisel,** 1882
Metal and wood. 8 3/4″ x 1 1/2″
Harvard C. Wood, III

31. **Caliper,** 1890
Metal. 11″ x 6″ x 1/4″
Harvard C. Wood, III

32. **Surface grinder,** 1920
Metal. 4 3/4″ x 4″
Harvard C. Wood, III

33. **Glue pot,** 1920
Metal. 4 3/4″ (diameter) x 3 3/4″
Harvard C. Wood, III

34. **Glue pot ladel,** 1920
Metal. 3 1/2″ x 9″ x 2″
Harvard C. Wood, III

35. **Assorted letters,** 1922
Metal and lead. 2″ x 2″ x 1/4″
Harvard C. Wood, III

36. **Sandblasting dope (1 brick),** 1928
Resin. 11″ x 5 1/2 ″ x 2″
Harvard C. Wood, III

37. **Abrasive for grinding and polishing,** 1920s
Metal grain (1 pound)
Harvard C. Wood, III

38. **Electric glue pot,** 1930
Metal. 9″ (diameter) x 10″
Harvard C. Wood, III

39. **Sand blasting nozzles,** c. 1930s
Metal. 2 1/2″ x 1 1/4″; 2 3/4″ x 1 1/2″;
4 1/2″ x 1 1/2″; 5″ x 2″
Harvard C. Wood, III

40. **Drill bit,** 1940
Metal. 5″ x 3/8″
Harvard C. Wood, III

41. **Cutting wheel,** 1940
Carborundum. 12 3/4″ (diameter)
Harvard C. Wood, III

42. **Face mask used for sandblasting,** 1940
Metal, plastic and cloth.
5 3/4″ x 3 1/2″
Harvard C. Wood, III

43. **Template,** 1988
Rubber. 11″ x 20″x 1/8″
Harvard C. Wood, III

44. **Sample abrasive used for sandblasting,** 1988
Metal grain.
Harvard C. Wood, III

45. **Cutting bits,** 1988
Metal. 5/8″ x 3 1/4″ x 5/8″;
1/2″ x 2 1/2″ x 1/2″;
1/2″ x 5 3/4″ x 1/2″;
1 1/8″ x 6 3/8″ x 5/8″;
5/8″ x 3″ x 5/8″
Harvard C. Wood, III

46. **Face mask,** 1988
Cloth. 5 1/4″ x 5″ x 3″
Balch Institute for Ethnic Studies

47. **Company ledger used by** Harvard C. Wood, Lansdowne, 1923-1925
Cloth binding and paper.
10 1/2″ x 8″
Harvard C. Wood, III

Skills

48. Trail bag by Robert C. Moore, Boalsburg, 1988
Lenni Lenape
Squirrel skin and deer hide, decorated with wampum beads
17″ x 8 1/2″
Robert C. Moore

49. Belt with buckle by Robert C. Moore, Boalsburg, 1988
Lenni Lenape
Leather and beads
Belt: 34″ x 1 1/4″
Buckle: 4″ x 2 3/4″
Robert C. Moore

50. Ceremonial fan by Robert C. Moore, Boalsburg, 1988
Lenni Lenape
Turkey wing and wampum beads
26″ x 4 1/2″
Robert C. Moore

51. Knife sheath by Robert C. Moore, Boalsburg, 1988
Lenni Lenape
Moose hide and wampum beads
2 1/2″ x 6 1/4″ x 3/4″
Robert C. Moore

52. Knife by Robert C. Moore, Boalsburg, 1988
Lenni Lenape
Flint blade on deer legbone.
6 1/4″ x 1 1/4″
Robert C. Moore

53. Moccasins by Robert C. Moore, Boalsburg, 1988
Lenni Lenape
Deerskin, porcupine quills and deer hair. Each 10″ x 4″
Robert C. Moore

54. Breechcloth by Robert C. Moore, Boalsburg, 1988
Lenni Lenape
Deerskin. 60″ x 9 1/4″
Robert C. Moore

55. Shirt with cape by Robert C. Moore, Boalsburg, 1988
Lenni Lenape
Deerskin with cowrie shells, wampum and muskrat jaws
Shirt: 17″ x 28 1/2″ x 1/16″
Cape: 26″ x 16 1/2″ x 1/16″
Robert C. Moore

56. Leggings with finger-woven belt by Robert C. Moore, Boalsburg, 1988
Lenni Lenape
Deerskin
Leggings: Each: 31 1/4″ x 15 1/2″
Belt: 41″ x 7/8″
Robert C. Moore

57. Pair of garter tabs by Robert C. Moore, Boalsburg, 1988
Lenni Lenape
Deerskin and porcupine quills
28″ x 2″ x 1/16″
Robert C. Moore

58. Medicine bag ("puzzle pouch") by Robert C. Moore, Boalsburg, 1988
Iroquois
Leather and beads. 7 3/4″ x 3″
Robert C. Moore.

Crafting Sound

59. "Double Tenor" drum pans by Terrence Cameron, Philadelphia, 1988
Afro-Caribbean
Carborundum steel.
22 1/2″ (diameter) x 6 1/4″
Terrence Cameron

60. *Cuatro* by Aguedo Beltran, Philadelphia, 1988
Puerto Rican
Black walnut, spruce, ebony and mahogany. 34 1/4″ x 10 1/4″ x 3 1/2″
Aguedo Beltran

61. *Prim* by Frank Valentich, Pittsburgh, 1988
Croatian
Maple, spruce and poplar.
24 1/2″ x 6 1/4″ x 1 1/2″
Tuning, from highest to lowest strings: D-D-A-E-B
Balch Institute for Ethnic Studies

Creating Community

62. "Laurel Wreath" quilt by Fonda Smith, Pittsburgh, 1983-1984
Irish, English, German, Dutch, French. 74″ x 98″
Fonda Smith

63. Unfinished "Pinwheels" by Robbie Seibert, Sheila Graham and Fonda Smith, Pittsburgh, 1988
Irish, English, German, Dutch, French
Single block cotton, pieced and quilted. 14 1/2″ x 15 1/2″
Allison Park Quiltmakers

64. "Bluebird" appliqué by Mary Margaret Sullivan, Pittsburgh, 1988
Design copyrighted by Nancy Pearson
Irish
Single block cotton. 18″ x 18″
Mary Margaret Sullivan

65. Victorian "Crazy Patch" by Fonda Smith, Pittsburgh, 1988
Irish, English, German, Dutch, French
Pieced cotton with embroidery and appliqué. 11 1/4″ x 11 1/4″
Fonda Smith

66. Diagram of piecing for "Crazy Patch" quilt block, Pittsburgh, 1988
Paper. 8 1/2″ x 11″
Allison Park Quiltmakers

67. "Double-Four" quilt block by Lucille Cardone, Pittsburgh, 1988
Italian
Pieced cotton. 12 1/4″ x 12 1/4″
Allison Park Quiltmakers

68. Diagram of piecing for "Double-Four" quilt block, Pittsburgh, 1988
Paper. 8 1/2″ x 11″
Allison Park Quiltmakers

69. "Baby Bud" quilt block by Mary Lou Wolff, Pittsburgh, 1988
German, Irish
Pieced cotton. 12″ x 11 3/4″
Allison Park Quiltmakers

70.   Diagram of piecing for "Baby Bud" quilt block, Pittsburgh, 1988
Paper. 8 1/2" x 11"
Allison Park Quiltmakers

71.   "Card Tricks" quilt block by Robbie Seibert, Pittsburgh, 1988
German, English
Pieced cotton. 12 1/4" x 12 1/4"
Allison Park Quiltmakers

72.   Diagram of piecing for "Card Tricks" quilt block, Pittsburgh, 1988
Paper. 8 1/2" x 11"
Allison Park Quiltmakers

73.   Piecing templates for "Card Tricks" quilt block, Pittsburgh, 1988
Plastic. 4 3/4" x 6 1/2"; 5" x 3 1/2"
Allison Park Quiltmakers

74.   Quilting template ("Squiggle" pattern), Pittsburgh, 1982
Cardboard. 7" x 2 1/2"
Allison Park Quiltmakers

75.   Quilting templates ("Interlocking Circles" pattern), Pittsburgh, 1982
Plastic and wood. 14 1/2" x 2 1/2"; 15 1/2" x 2 1/2"
Allison Park Quiltmakers

76.   Quilting template ("Interlocking Diamonds" pattern), Pittsburgh, 1982
Plastic. 9" x 2 1/2"
Allison Park Quiltmakers

77.   Quilting template, ("Hawaiian" pattern), Pittsburgh, 1986
Plastic ("shrinky-dink") and sandpaper. 6 1/2" x 5"
Allison Park Quiltmakers

78.   Knife by Bob Rock, Everett, 1988
Wood and metal. 11 1/2" x 3/4"
Bob Rock

79.   Saw blades used for making knife blades
a) 10 1/4" x 1 1/2"
b) 11 3/4" x 2"
c) 10 3/8" x 2 1/4"
Bob Rock

80.   Hand saw sharpening jig by Bob Rock, Everett, c. 1965
Wood. 25" x 2 1/4" x 1 1/2"
Bob Rock

81.   Banjo pot by Bob Rock, Everett, 1988
Wood. 10 1/2" (diameter) x 6" x 1/4"
Bob Rock

82.   Banjo rim by Bob Rock, Everett, 1988
Iron. 11 1/2" (diameter) x 1/2"
Bob Rock

83.   Banjo neck (in the rough) by Bob Rock, Everett, 1988
Wood. 29 1/4" x 4" x 2 1/4"
Bob Rock

84.   Pattern for banjo fret board by Bob Rock, Everett, 1988
Wood. 20 1/8" x 1 3/4"
Bob Rock

85.   Resonator ring by Bob Rock, Everett, 1988
Metal. 13 1/2" (diameter) x 1 1/2"
Bob Rock

86.   Resonator (without bottom wood) by Bob Rock, Everett, 1988
Metal. 13 1/4" x 5 1/4" x 1/4"
Bob Rock

87.   Banjo by Bob Rock, Everett, early 1970s
Wood and metal
13 1/2" x 34 3/4" x 3 1/2"
Darrell G. Spencer

88.   Welded chain by Bob Rock, Everett, 1988
Metal. 3'
Bob Rock

89.   Hickory rocker by Lee Woida, Fairhope, 1988
Hickory and oak. 30" x 44" x 36"
Balch Institute for Ethnic Studies

90.   Miniature hickory rocker by Lee Woida, Fairhope, 1988
Hickory and oak.
7 1/2" x 11 1/2" x 9 7/8"
Lee Woida

91.   Jig for bending back slats of rocker by Lee Woida, Fairhope, 1988
Wood and metal. 42" x 42" x 15"
Lee Woida

92.   Seat slats and slat support by Lee Woida, 1988
Oak
Slats: 20" x 1 3/4"; 35" x 1 1/4"
Support: 17" x 1" x 1 1/8"
Lee Woida

93.   Side wrap-arounds and back ring by Lee Woida, Fairhope, 1988
Hickory. 12" x 1"
Lee Woida

94.   Seat loop and kidney by Lee Woida, Fairhope, 1988
Loop (oak): 19" x 19"
Kidney (hickory): 19 1/2" x 14"
Lee Woida

95.   Front panel of seat loop (unnotched) by Lee Woida, Fairhope, 1988
Oak. 20" x 1 1/2" x 5/8"
Lee Woida

96.   Arm and front leg by Lee Woida, Fairhope, 1988
Hickory. 29" x 15"; 27" x 17"
Lee Woida

97.   Back leg piece by Lee Woida, Fairhope, 1988
Hickory. 40" x 1 1/4"
Lee Woida

98.   Rocker piece by Lee Woida, Fairhope, 1988
Hickory. 34 1/2" x 1" x 1 1/2"
Lee Woida

Values and Beliefs

99. Looped piece by Lee Woida, Fairhope, 1988
Hickory. 26″ x 22″
Lee Woida

100. Latshaw Furniture catalog, 1988
Printed on paper. 8 1/2″ x 11″
Pennsylvania Heritage Affairs Commission

101. *Summer Wheat Harvest* by Aaron Zook, Kinzers, 1988
Three-dimensional carved painting using a variety of materials
20″ x 32″ x 3 1/2″
Aaron Zook

102. *Fall Corn Husking* by Aaron Zook, Kinzers, 1988
Three-dimensional carved painting using a variety of materials
20″ x 32″ x 3 1/2″
Aaron Zook

103. Hooked rug, Rug Making Shop, Lancaster County, 1987
Old Order Amish
Wool. 38 1/4″ x 27″ x 3/8″
Balch Institute for Ethnic Studies

104. Front and rear wheel rim and spokes, Spokes and Rims Shop, Lancaster County, 1988
Old Order Amish
Hickory
Rims: 40″ x 11 1/2″ x 1″
Spokes: 22″ x 3/4″
Balch Institute for Ethnic Studies

105. Shaft, Wood Bending Shop, Lancaster County, 1988
Old Order Mennonite
Steamed and bent hickory
7′4″ x 1 3/4″
Balch Institute for Ethnic Studies

106. Front and rear axles, Axle Shop, Lancaster County, 1988
Old Order Mennonite
Metal. 5′8″ x 1″ x 1″
Balch Institute for Ethnic Studies

107. Front and rear axle beds, Carriage and Woodworking Shop, Lancaster County, 1988
Old Order Mennonite
Hickory. 4′ 6 1/4″ x 1 3/4″ x 1 1/2″;
4′ 6 1/4″ x 2 1/4″ x 1″
Balch Institute for Ethnic Studies

108. Single-Tree, Carriage and Woodworking Shop, Lancaster County, 1988
Old Order Mennonite
Hickory and metals
39 1/2″ x 2″ x 1 1/2″
Balch Institute for Ethnic Studies

109. Head block, Carriage and Woodworking Shop, Lancaster County, 1988
Old Order Mennonite
Hickory. 17 1/4″ x 1 1/2″ x 1 3/8″
Balch Institute for Ethnic Studies

110. Spring bar, Carriage and Woodworking Shop, Lancaster County, 1988
Old Order Mennonite
Hickory. 38 1/2″ x 2 ″ x 1 1/2″
Balch Institute for Ethnic Studies

111. Lamp (complete), Carriage Shop, Lancaster County, 1988
Old Order Amish
Metal, glass, painted brass, and plastic. 4 1/4″ x 5 1/4″
Balch Institute for Ethnic Studies

112. Lamp shell, Coach Restoration Shop, Lancaster County, 1988
Spun brass.
4 1/4″ (diameter) x 2 2/16″
Balch Institute for Ethnic Studies

113. Lamp shell (with props), Coach Restoration Shop, Lancaster County, 1988
Brass. 5 1/4″ x 2 2/16″
Balch Institute for Ethnic Studies

114. Lamp shell (painted, with props), Coach Restoration Shop, Lancaster County, 1988
Brass and wire. 5 1/4″ x 2 2/16″
Balch Institute for Ethnic Studies

115. Lamp prop, Coach Restoration Shop, Lancaster County, 1988
Metal. 1 3/16″ x 1 1/2″
Balch Institute for Ethnic Studies

116. **Lamp plug,** Coach Restoration Shop, Lancaster County, 1988
Plastic and metal. 1 3/4″ x 3/4″
Balch Institute for Ethnic Studies

117. **Lamp lens,** Coach Restoration Shop, Lancaster County, 1988
Glass. 3 1/4″ (diameter) x 1 1/2″
Balch Institute for Ethnic Studies

118. **Lamp lens ring,** Coach Restoration Shop, Lancaster County, 1988
Metal. 3 1/4″ x 1/4″
Balch Institute for Ethnic Studies

119. **Lamp socket and flasherholder,** Coach Restoration Shop, Lancaster County, 1988
Wire, glass, and metal
4 1/2″ (diameter)
Balch Institute for Ethnic Studies

120. **Seal beam ring,** Coach Restoration Shop, Lancaster County, 1988
Metal. 4 3/4″ x 1/2″
Balch Institute for Ethnic Studies

121. **Fifth wheel,** Fifth Wheel Shop, Lancaster County, 1988
Old Order Mennonite
Metal. 14 3/4″ x 14 3/4″ x 2 1/2″
Balch Institute for Ethnic Studies

122. **Piece of carriage body,** Carriage Body Shop, Lancaster County, 1988
Old Order Amish
Fiberglass. 15″ x 4″
Balch Institute for Ethnic Studies

123. **Axle setting gauge for carriage,** Axle Shop, Lancaster County, 1988
Old Order Mennonite
Metal. 5′7″ x 9″ x 4″
Balch Institute for Ethnic Studies

124. **Carriage body rolling tools,** Carriage Body Shop, Lancaster County, 1988
Metal and wood
13″ x 7″; 10 1/2″ x 1 3/4″
Balch Institute for Ethnic Studies

125. **Harness and tack,** Harness Shop, Lancaster County, Old Order Amish
Leather
12″ x 36″ x 12″; 24″ x 90″ x 4″
Balch Institute for Ethnic Studies

126. **Battery,** Battery Shop, Lancaster County, 1988
Old Order Amish
Plastic casing, lead plates
10″ x 8 1/4″ x 6 1/2″
Balch Institute for Ethnic Studies

127. **Apron,** Tailoring Shop, Lancaster County, 1987
Old Order Amish
Polyester. 32 1/2″ x 5′ 2 1/2″
Balch Institute for Ethnic Studies

128. **Dress,** Tailoring Shop, Lancaster County, 1987
Old Order Amish
Polyester. 43″ x 31″ (waist 15 1/2″)
Balch Institute for Ethnic Studies

129. **Cap,** Tailoring Shop, Lancaster County, 1987
Old Order Amish
Organdy. 8 1/2″ x 7″ x 2 1/2″
Balch Institute for Ethnic Studies

130. **Hat,** Tailoring Shop, Lancaster County, 1987
Old Order Amish
Felt and ribbon. 4 1/2″ x 13 5/8″ x 15″
Balch Institute for Ethnic Studies

131. **Shirt,** Tailoring Shop, Lancaster County, 1987
Old Order Amish
Polyester. 30 1/2″ x 57″
Balch Institute for Ethnic Studies

132. ***Mutze*** (suit jacket), Tailoring Shop, Lancaster County, 1987
Old Order Amish
Polyester. 30 3/4″ x 40 1/2″
Balch Institute for Ethnic Studies

133. **Suit vest,** Tailoring Shop, Lancaster County, 1987
Old Order Amish
Polyester. 24″ x 38″
Balch Institute for Ethnic Studies

134. **Suit pants,** Tailoring Shop, Lancaster County, 1987
Old Order Amish
Polyester. 39 3/4″ x 34″
Balch Institute for Ethnic Studies

135. **Suspenders,** Tailoring Shop, Lancaster County, 1987
Old Order Amish
Elastic. 36″ x 8 1/2″
Balch Institute for Ethnic Studies

136. *Paska* (eggbread) by Marijka
Jula, Carnegie, 1988
Ukrainian
Shellacked, braided dough
5″ x 4 1/2″
Jula Family

137. *Servetka* (ritual cloth) by
Michael Jula, Carnegie, 1984
Ukrainian
Embroidered linen
14 1/2″ x 18 3/4″
Jula Family

138. Gilded candle, 1970
Ukrainian
Wax. 9 1/2″ x 1/2″
Kapeluck Family

139. *Krashanka* (ritual egg; typical
of all regions) by Kapeluck Family,
Carnegie, 1988
Ukrainian
Solid red. 2 7/16″ x 1 5/8″
Kapeluck Family

140. *Pysanka* (decorated egg),
"Oak Tree" (typical of Kiev region)
by Michael Kapeluck, Carnegie,
1987
Ukrainian
Red leaves on green background
2 7/16″ x 1 5/8″
Kapeluck Family

141. *Pysanka*, "Tear Drop" (typical
of Lemko region) by Michael Jula,
Carnegie, 1980s
Ukrainian
Red and white drops on green
background. 2 7/16″ x 1 5/8″
Jula Family

142. *Pysanka*, "Never-ending Line"
(typical of Hutsul region) by
Michael Kapeluck, Carnegie, 1987
Ukrainian
Orange, yellow and red waves
2 7/16″ x 1 5/8″
Kapeluck Family

143. *Pysanka*, "Greek Cross"
(typical of Hutsul region) by
Michael Kapeluck, Carnegie, 1987
Ukrainian
Red and yellow on brown
background. 2 7/16″ x 1 5/8″
Kapeluck Family

144. *Pysanka*, "Stags" (typical of
Hutsul region) by Michael
Kapeluck, Carnegie, 1987
Ukrainian
Brown, red and yellow
2 7/16″ x 1 5/8″
Kapeluck Family

145. *Pysanka*, "Geometric" with
cross and star symbol (typical of
Bukovina region) by Michael
Kapeluck, Carnegie, 1987
Ukrainian
2 7/16″ x 1 5/8″
Kapeluck Family

146. *Pysanka*, "Ikon of St. Michael"
(modern style) by Michael
Kapeluck, Carnegie, 1985
Ukrainian
2 7/16″ x 1 5/8″
Kapeluck Family

147. Six eggs showing stages in
the "wax resist" production
process. "Eight-point star"
design by Michael Kapeluck,
Carnegie, 1988
Ukrainian
Each 2 7/16″ x 1 5/8″
Kapeluck Family

148. *Kistka* (stylus) by Stephen
Kapeluck, Carnegie, 1988
Ukrainian
Pussywillow stick with a pin
6 5/8″ x 1/8″
Kapeluck Family

149. *Kistka* by Stephen Kapeluck,
Carnegie, 1988
Ukrainian
Pencil with a pin. 7 1/2″ x 1/4″
Kapeluck Family

150. *Kistka*, 1980s
Ukrainian
Pussywillow stick with copper-
wired funnel. 4 3/4″ x 1″
Kapeluck Family

151. *Kistka*, Johnson City, New
York, 1960s
Ukrainian
Wooden stick with embedded
metal funnel. 4 1/16″ x 11/16″
Kapeluck Family

152. *Kistka*, 1980s
Ukrainian
Plastic handle with metal funnel
5 1/4″ x 5/8″
Kapeluck Family

153. Dish of undyed beeswax for
liquefying (for Lemko style eggs)
by Kapeluck family, Carnegie,
1988
Ukrainian
Smooth, rose-beige wax
3 1/2″ x 5/8″
Kapeluck Family

154. Dish of undyed beeswax for
liquefying (for Hutsul and other
"wax resist" style eggs) by
Kapeluck family, Carnegie, 1988
Lumpy, carbon center, golden
periphery. 3 1/4″ x 7/8″
Kapeluck Family

155. Chunk of undyed beeswax
(irregular), 1980s
Ukrainian
4 3/4″ x 1 1/2″
Kapeluck Family

156. Undyed beeswax blocks,
1980s
Ukrainian
Square with molded pattern
1 3/4″ x 1 3/4″ x 9/16″
Kapeluck Family

157. Undyed beeswax block
(blackened from use), 1960s
Ukrainian
Square. 1 5/8″ x 1 5/8″ x 1/2″
Kapeluck Family

158. Dyed beeswax block
(blackened from further use),
1970s
Ukrainian
Square. 1 1/16″ x 1 1/16″ x 1/2″
Kapeluck Family

159. *Hlab pav duav* (sash),
Thailand, 1979
Hmong
Dacron polyester. 5′ x 19″ x 1/16″
Pang Xiong Sirirathasuk

160. *Nroob nrag* (anklets) by Pang
Xiong Sirirathasuk, Philadelphia,
1980
Hmong
Cotton, satin, wool braid, polyester
braid, and cotton pom-poms
7″ x 8 3/4″ (bottom) x 13″ (top)
Pang Xiong Sirirathasuk

161. Coin purses by Bao Yang, Sr.
and Bao Yang, Jr., Philadelphia
and Thailand, 1985-1987
Hmong
Cotton, acetate blend; silver and
plastic. 27″ x 9 1/2″ x 1/2″
Bao Yang

162. *Paj ntaub* ("flower cloth"),
maze pattern; *dab tshos* collar
design Thailand, 1984
Hmong
Cotton blend. 41″ x 39 1/4″
Margaret Mills

163. "New Style" *sev* (front and
back panel and sash) by Mai Doua
Moua, France, 1984
Hmong
Embossed velvet; woven and
sequined braid; acetate
11′ 4″ x 2′ 10 1/2″ x 1/8″
Lhee Moua Sirirathasuk

164. "New Style" *tsha* (jacket) and
dab tshos (collar) by Mai Doua
Moua, France, 1984
Hmong
Embossed velvet; acetate blends;
sequin braid. 34″ x 21″ x 1/4″
Lhee Moua Sirirathasuk

165. Neckpiece by Neng Vang
Siong, Thailand, 1984
Hmong
Aluminum. 16 5/8″ x 12 1/2″ x 3/4″
Lhee Moua Sirirathasuk

166. Flower hat by Lue Moua,
California, 1984
Hmong
Cotton, sequin braid, spangles and
pompom braid
8″ x 11 1/2″ x 1/2″
Pa Houa Moua Yang

167. Blouse by Thong Lor,
Thailand, c. 1983
Hmong
Polyester blend and rayon
23″ x 24″ x 1/8″
Mai Vang Chang

168. Scarf
Polyester blend. 27 1/2″ x 27 1/2″
Mai Vang Chang

169. Green Hmong *thiab* (skirt) by
Mao Nyia Xiong, Thailand, 1981
Hmong
Cotton & acetate ribbon with batik,
applique, and embroidery
25″ x 38″ x 1/2″
Mai Vang Chang

170. *Paj ntaub* ("story cloth")
illustrating the escape of the
Hmong from persecution in Laos,
the journey to the refugee camps
in Thailand and subsequent
resettlement to the United States,
by Youa Vang, Thailand, 1986
Hmong
Cotton and cotton/synthetic blend
66″ x 78 5/8″ x 1/8″
Pang Xiong Sirirathasuk

171. *Paj ntaub* ("flower cloth"),
"Protective Cross with Snails"
design, by Mao Moua, Coatesville,
1986
Hmong
Cotton and cotton blends, wood
and metal embroidery hoop with
lace frame. 15″ x 1/2″
Sally Peterson

172. Apprenticeship Sampler
Quilt, by Pang Xiong Sirirathasuk,
Yee Vang Lo, Mao Vang Xiong, Yer
Lo, Mai Xiong Chang, Pa Houa
Moua, Ka Xiong, Bao Yang, Foua
Lo, Lhee Moua Sirirathasuk, Yer
Xiong, Shai Yang, and assembled
by Pang Xiong Sirirathasuk,
Philadelphia, 1987
Hmong
Cotton and cotton blend
50 3/8″ x 58 3/8″ x 1/8″
Pang Xiong Sirirathasuk

173. Pack basket by Chia Ker Lor,
Thailand, 1980
Hmong
Bamboo. 16 3/4″ x 14″ (top);
10″ x 4″ (bottom)
Chia Ker Lor

174. Rice winnower by Chia Ker
Lor, Philadelphia, 1987
Hmong
Plastic coil strapping on wood
frame. 23 3/4″ (diameter) x 3/4″
Chia Ker Lor

175. "Two Birds," hex sign by Bill
Schuster, Emmaus, 1988
Pennsylvania German
Painted wood. 18" (diameter)
Bill and Charlotte Schuster

176. "Wilkum 1969," hex sign by
Bill Schuster, Emmaus, 1988
Pennsylvania German
Painted wood. 20" (diameter)
Thomas E. Graves

177. "Hearts and Star," hex sign by
Bill Schuster, Emmaus, 1988
Pennsylvania German
Painted wood. 20" (diameter)
Bill and Charlotte Schuster

178. "Angel with Tulip and Double
Rosette," hex sign by Ivan Hoyt,
Wapwallopen, 1988
Pennsylvania German
Painted wood. 16" (diameter)
Ivan E. Hoyt

179. "Two Deer with 'Spinning'
Rosettes," hex sign by Ivan Hoyt,
Wapwallopen, 1988
Pennsylvania German
Painted wood. 24" (diameter)
Ivan E. Hoyt

180. "Double Distlefink with 'hill'
border," hex sign by Ivan Hoyt,
Wapwallopen, 1988
Pennsylvania German
Painted wood. 24" (diameter)
Ivan E. Hoyt

181. "Tree-of-Life" (2 birds), hex
sign by John Claypoole,
Lenhartsville, 1987
Pennsylvania German
Painted wood. 16" (diameter)
John Claypoole

182. "Sun and Rain" (Star), hex sign
by John Claypoole, Lenhartsville,
1987
Pennsylvania German
Painted wood. 24" (diameter)
John Claypoole

183. "Wilkom," hex sign by John
Claypoole, Lenhartsville, 1986
Pennsylvania German
Painted wood. 15 1/2" (diameter)
John Claypoole

184. "Calico Star," hex sign by
John Claypoole, Lenhartsville,
1989
Pennsylvania German
Painted wood. 3' (diameter)
Balch Institute for Ethnic Studies

185. Dish attributed to John Leidy,
Sr., Hilltown Township, Bucks
County, 1796
Pennsylvania German
Inscribed: "es ist kein voglein so
vergesen es ruth ein studndlein
nach dem esen geschehen den 20
ichsten Nofember 1796" ("No bird is
so entirely forgetful that it does not
rest a short while after eating.
Happened the 20th of November
1796.")
Wheel-thrown redware. Surface
covered with white slip daubed
with copper oxide (green). *Sgraffito*
banding and decoration
Yellowish lead glaze
13 1/4" (diameter) x 2 1/2"
Philadelphia Museum of Art. Gift of
John T. Morris. 00-70

186. **Dish** by Lester Breininger,
Robesonia, 1985
Pennsylvania German
Modeled after 1796 dish by John
Leidy, Sr.
Inscribed "Not be ashamed I
Advise thee most if one learneth
thee what thou not Knowest the
Ingenious is Accounted Brave but
the Clumsey None Desire to have"
Inscribed on back: "Breininger
Pottery/Robesonia, Pa/June 7,
1985/a very pleasant sunny day!"
Incised redware with yellow slip
and copper oxide decoration
17 1/2" (diameter) x 2 1/2"
Private Collection

187. *Fraktur* (birth certificate),
probably made in Lancaster
County, 1794-1800
Pennsylvania German
Inscribed for Johannes Axer, 1794
Translation: "I, Johannes Axer, was
conceived and born the 28th of
August, anno 1794, in the sign of
Capricorn in the year of our Lord
and Savior Jesus Christ. The Lord
of all lords bless and protect. To
God alone the glory. Let your
bearing constantly come under
this test: God sees, God hears,
God punishes; you will not escape
him. Pray without ceasing."
Ink with pigments in gum medium
on laid paper. 12 5/8" x 7 3/4"
Philadelphia Museum of Art.
Purchased. Special Museum Fund.
16-290

188. *Fraktur* (birth and baptismal
certificate) by Friedrich Krebs,
Dauphin County, 1790-1800
Pennsylvania German
Inscribed for Elizabeth
Kostenbader, born October 9,
1783.
Translation of main text: "To these
two married persons, namely
Henrich Kostenbader and his
lawful wife, Maria Christina, nee
Mayer, the daughter named
Elisabetha was born into the world
in the year of our Lord Jesus 1783
on the 9th day of October at __
o-clock in the sign of __. This
Elisabetha was born and baptised
in America in the state of
Pennsylvania in Northampton
County in Plainfield Township."
Watercolor wash and ink on laid
paper, relief printed with
letterpress.
16" x 13"
Philadelphia Museum of Art.
Bequest of Lisa Norris Elkins.
50-92-243

189. *Fraktur* (birth certificate), by
Ruthanne Hartung, Reading, 1987
Pennsylvania German
Inscribed for Edward James
Becker, born November 15, 1941 in
the county of Northampton in the
state of Pennsylvania
Watercolor wash and ink
16 1/8" x 13 1/8" x 1 1/8" (framed)
Balch Institute for Ethnic Studies

Photographs on the following pages are by:
Will Brown: cover: *prim,* 9, 10, 12, 13, 14, 15, 16, 17, 18, 19, 20, 21, 22, 23, 24, 25,
26, 27, 33, 45, 47, 66, 73, 77, 80 (top), 94, 95, 102, 108 (top), 109, 111, 119, 124
(top), 125, 129 (bottom)
Andrew Harkins/Philadelphia Museum of Art: 128
Anthony Kambic: 11, 68
Philadelphia Museum of Art: 124 (bottom)

Photographs on the following pages (from the Folklife Archives of the
Pennsylvania Heritage Affairs Commission, unless otherwise noted) are by:
Mai Xiong Chang: 108 (bottom)
Doris Dyen: 30, 58, 60, 64, 65, 100, 101, 103 (Photographs on pp. 58, 60, 64
and 65 were taken in conjunction with the "Neighborhood Traditions"
project, co-sponsored by The Carnegie Library and the Pennsylvania
Heritage Affairs Commission.)
J. Joseph Edgette: 38, 39 (top)
Thomas E. Graves: 7, 44
Michael E. Haritan: cover (Folk Festival)/courtesy of Chuck Cubelic
Susan L. F. Isaacs: 129 (top)
Geraldine Johnson: 83 (bottom)
Sally Peterson: 112, 113, 114, 116
John Reynolds: 50, 51, 52, 53, 54
Shalom Staub: 43, 81 (right), 115
Richard Vidutis: 80 (bottom), 81 (left), 82, 83 (top)
Mike Worley/Commonwealth Media Services: 8, 29, 31, 71, 72, 74, 75, 76, 89,
90, 91, 92, 93, 96
Unknown (from the H. C. Wood Family Archive): 36, 37, 39 (bottom), 40